AF322682

MY LITTLE BRAIN!

Explaining The Human Brain for Kids

BABY PROFESSOR

EDUCATION KIDS

LEARN ABOUT YOUR
BRAIN

The human
brain is like a
computer, but
a hundred times
more powerful.
It stores our
memory with
unlimited
capacity. Your
brain is the boss
of your body. It
runs the show
and controls
just about
everything
you do.

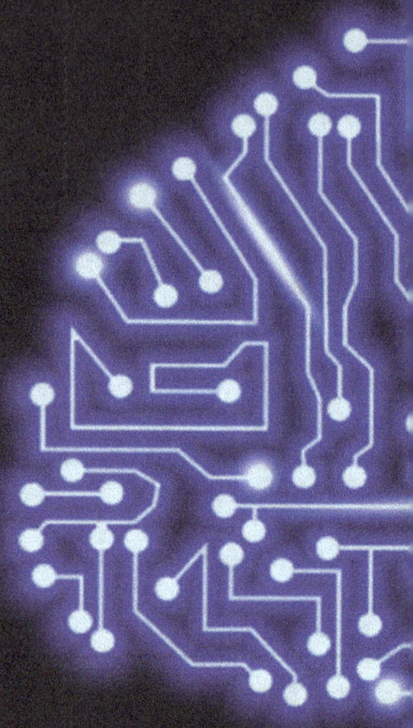

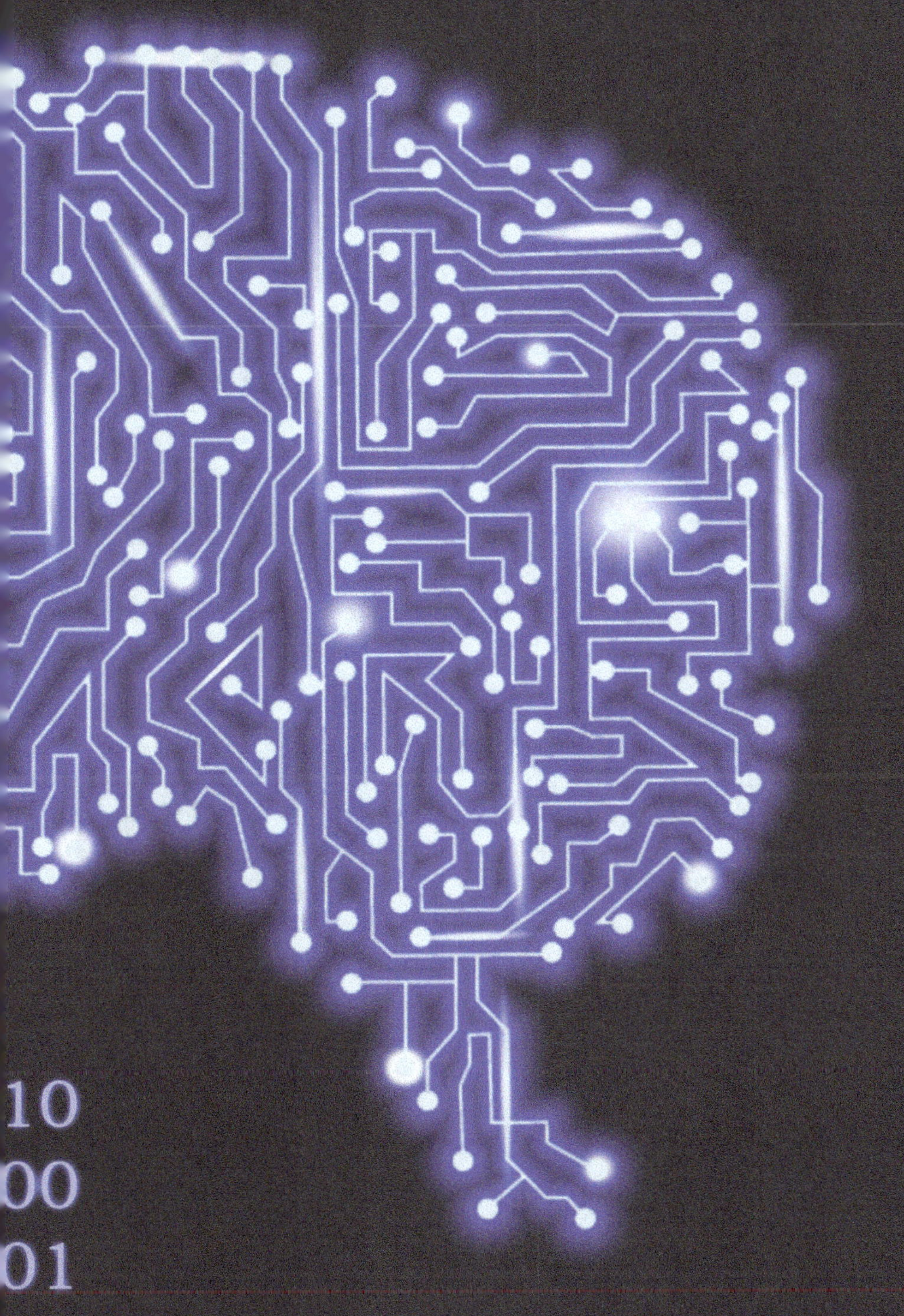
10
00
01

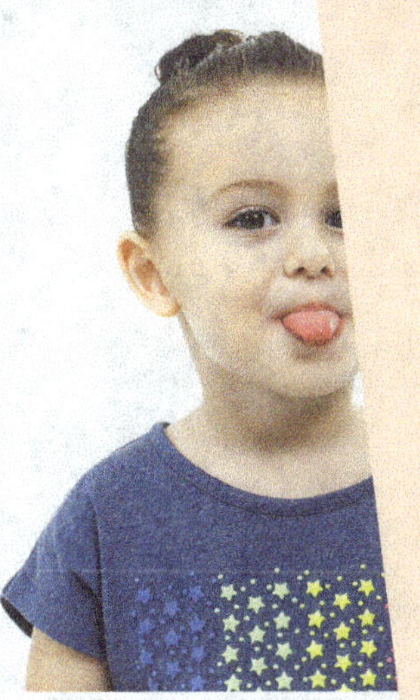

Your amazing brain controls every move you make and how you react. It controls you even when you're asleep. It allows you to feel emotions like happiness, sorrow, and anger.

The brain is a
powerful master
control panel.
The brain sends
the signals that
make your heart
beat, your lungs
draw in breath
and your eyelids
blink. It makes us
alive.

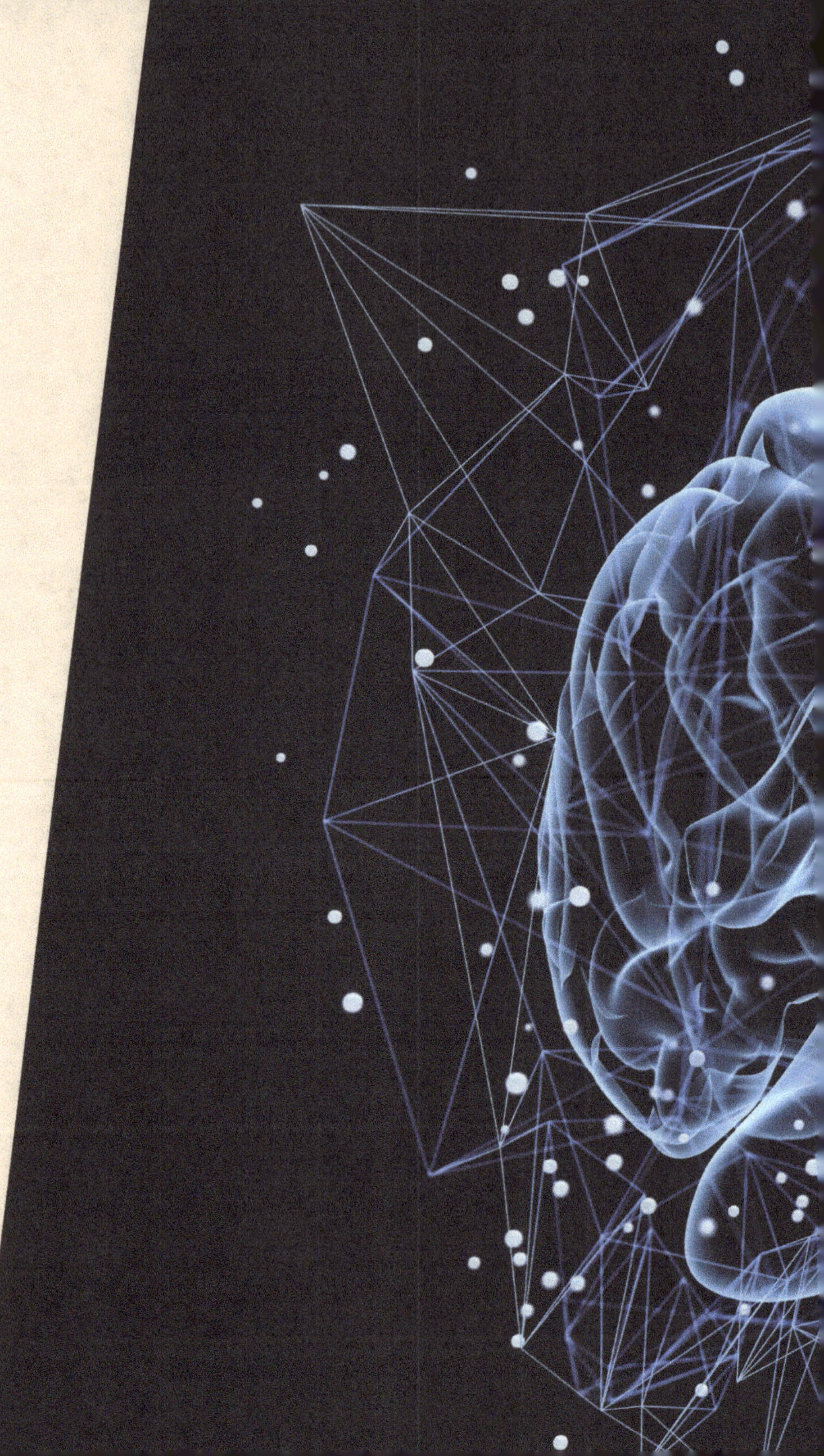

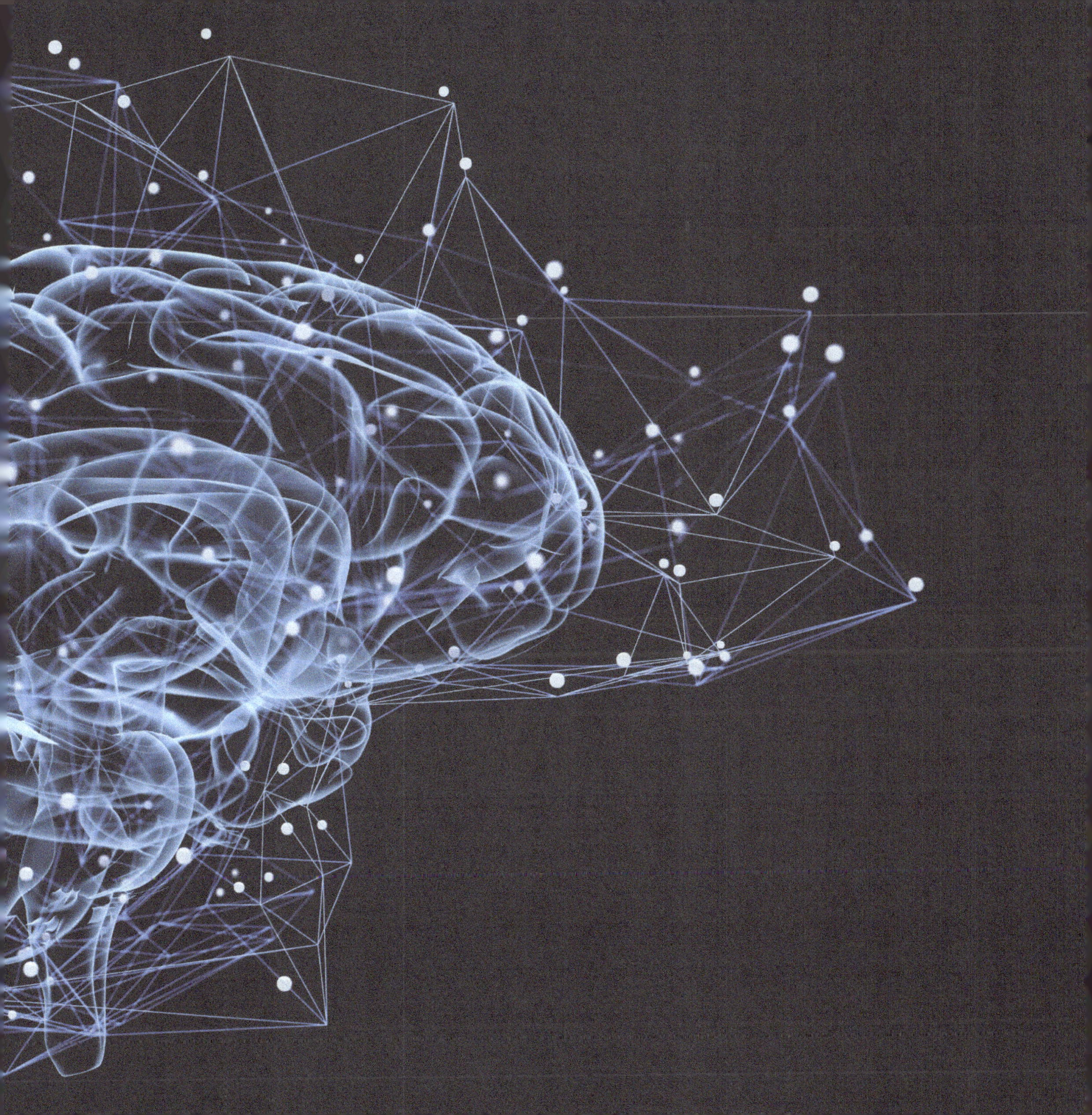

The three pound pink, wrinkly mass in your head might not look like much, but it has immense power, capacity and complexity that we still have not completely explored. It has evolved over time and features some incredibly intricate parts that have left scientists baffled for years.

The brain is
the center of
the human
nervous system.
There are
different parts
of the brain
that perform
particular
functions. It sits
in your skull at
the top of your
spinal cord.

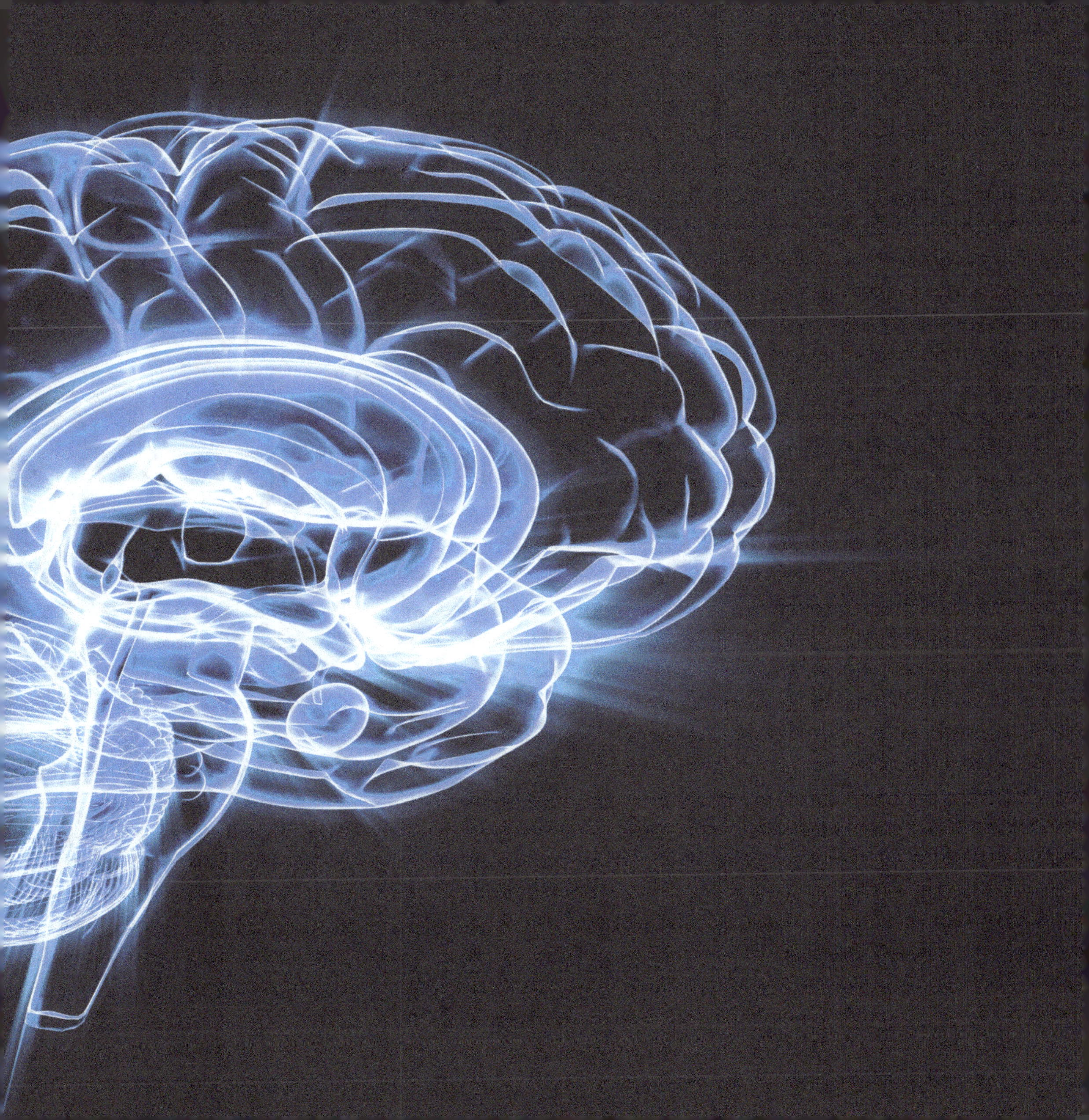

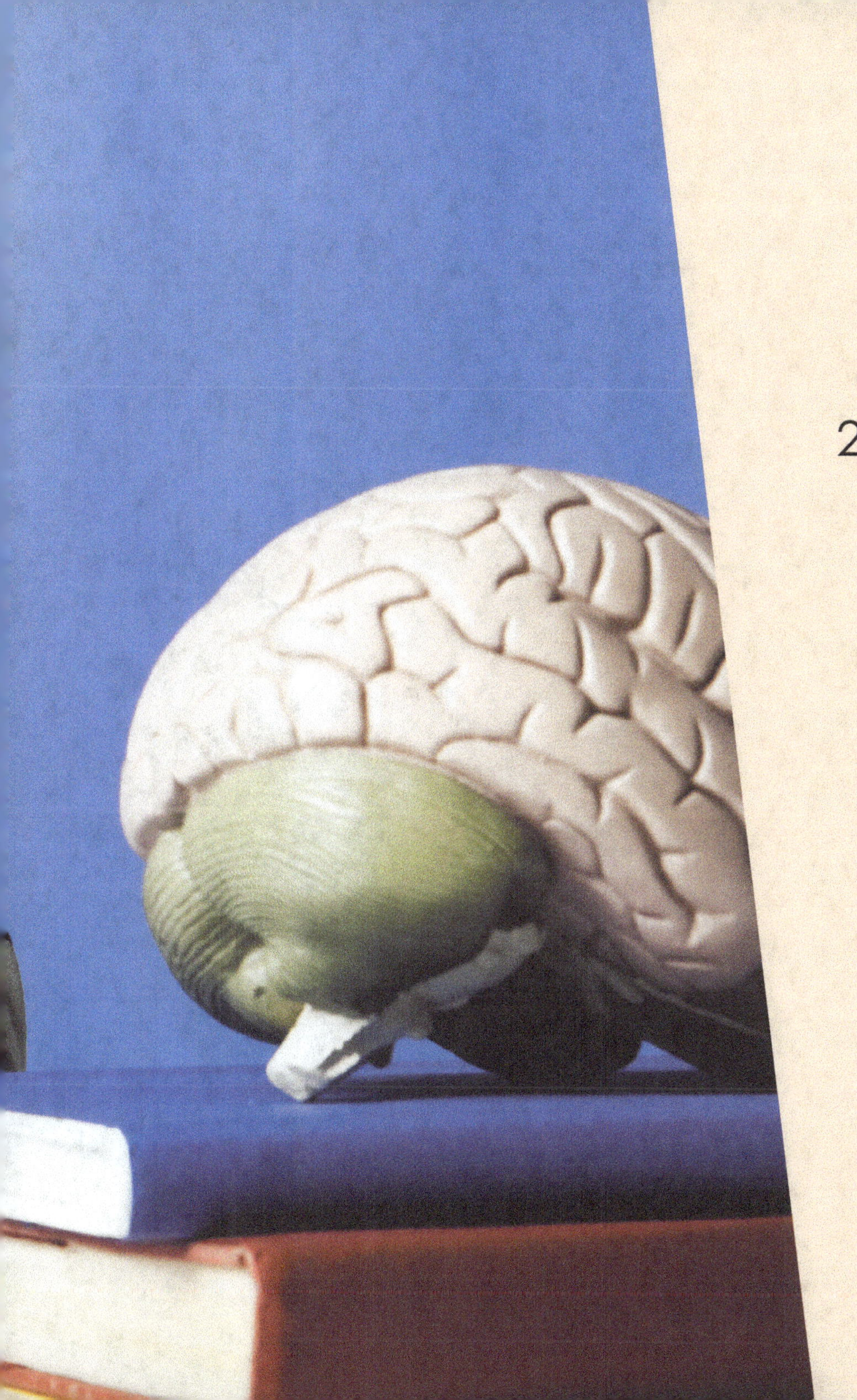

The brain is just
2% of your body
weight. It uses
around 20% of
all your energy
from the blood
and oxygen
in your body.
That's a lot for
such a small
organ.

Your brain
stops growing
around age
18. It continues
to work and
develop and
learn new
things. That
is why our
parents are
smart and why
we become
smarter as we
grow up.

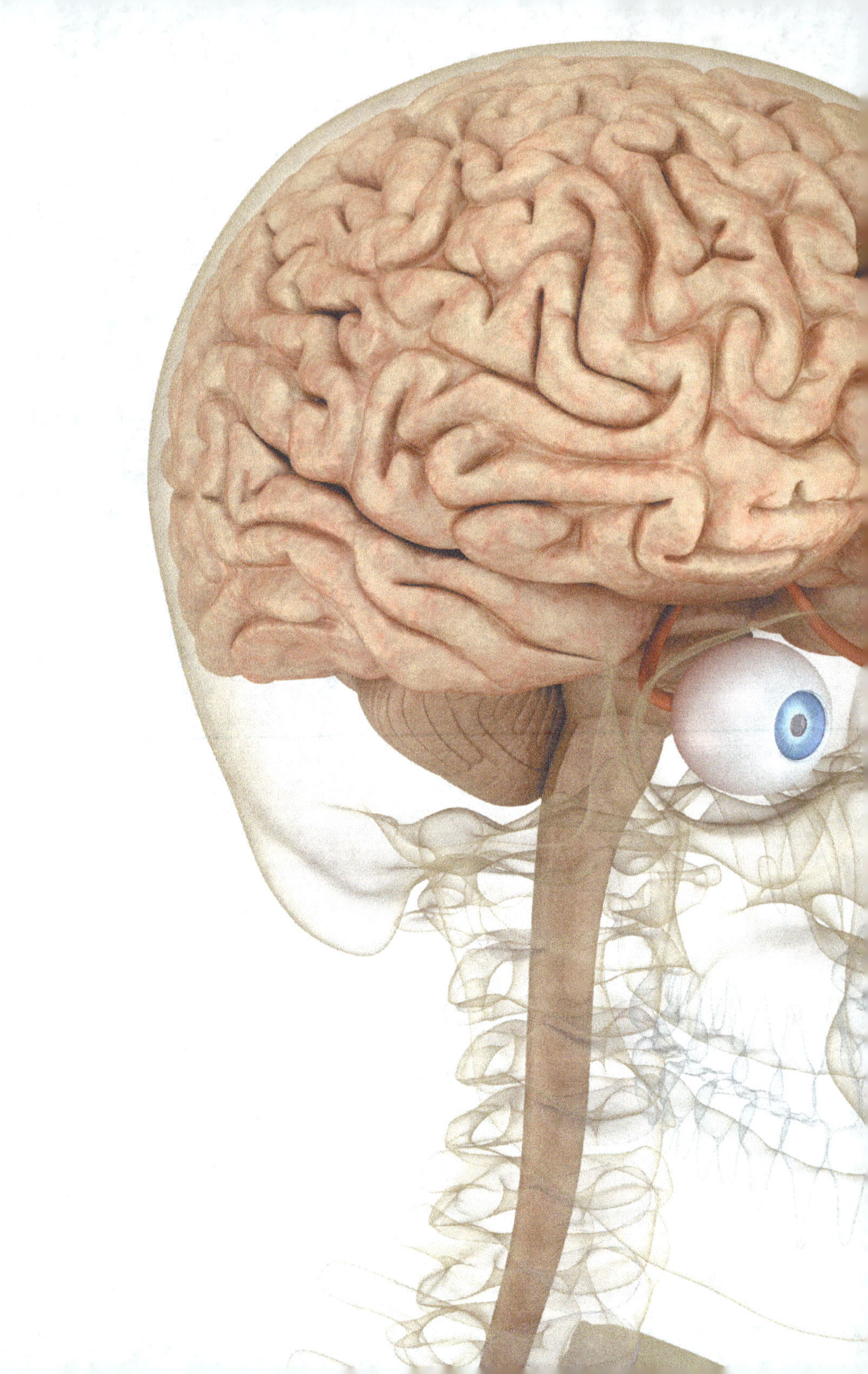

The brain of an adult human weighs around 3 pounds. The brain of an elephant is much larger than a human brain. Our brains are three times bigger than that of a chimpanzee.

The brain of an elephant only makes up 0.15% of their overall weight. When you compare it to our brains, which take up 2% of our body weight, humans still have the largest brain to body size. we're have the most brain power in relation to our size of any creature on Earth.

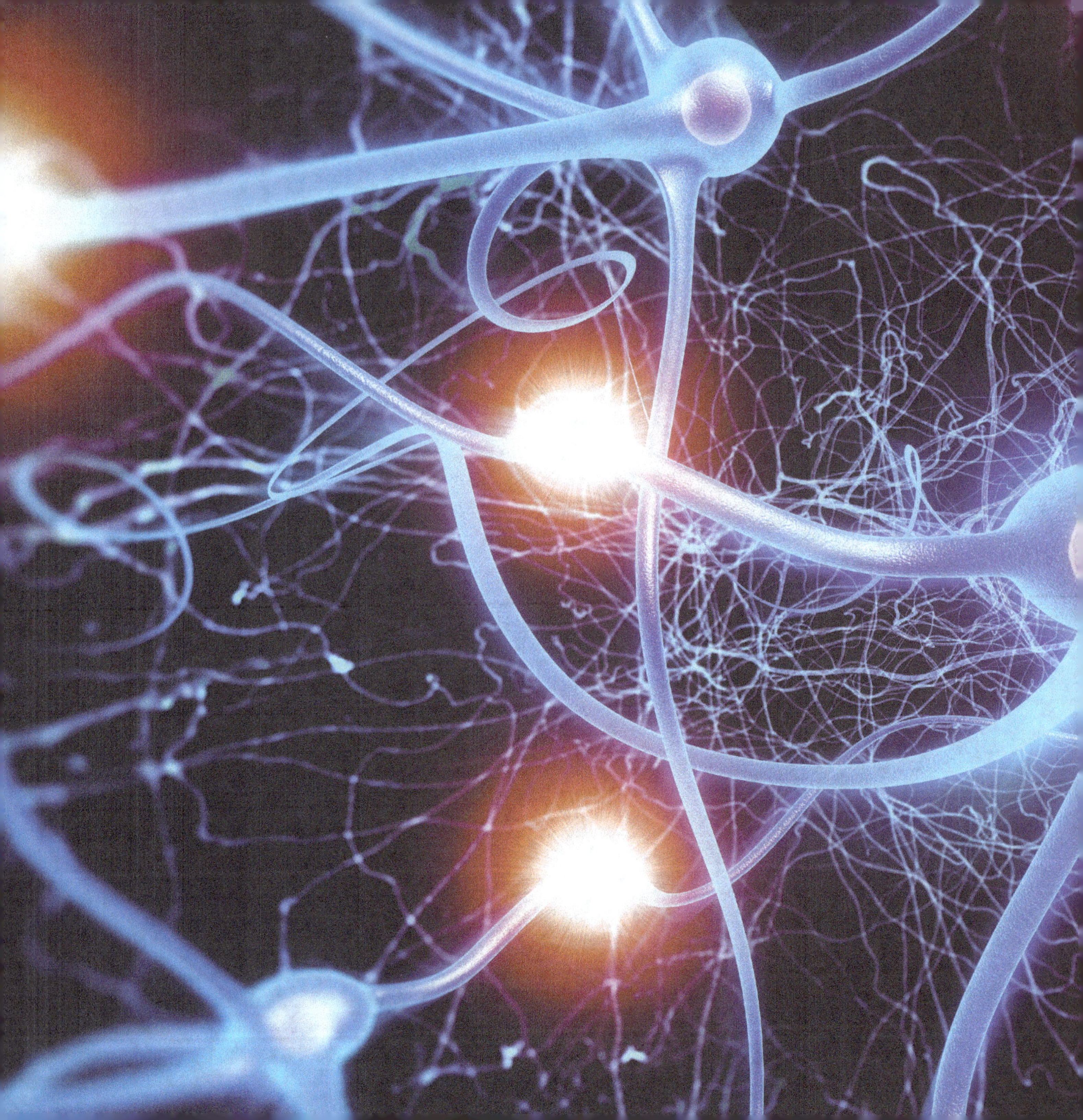

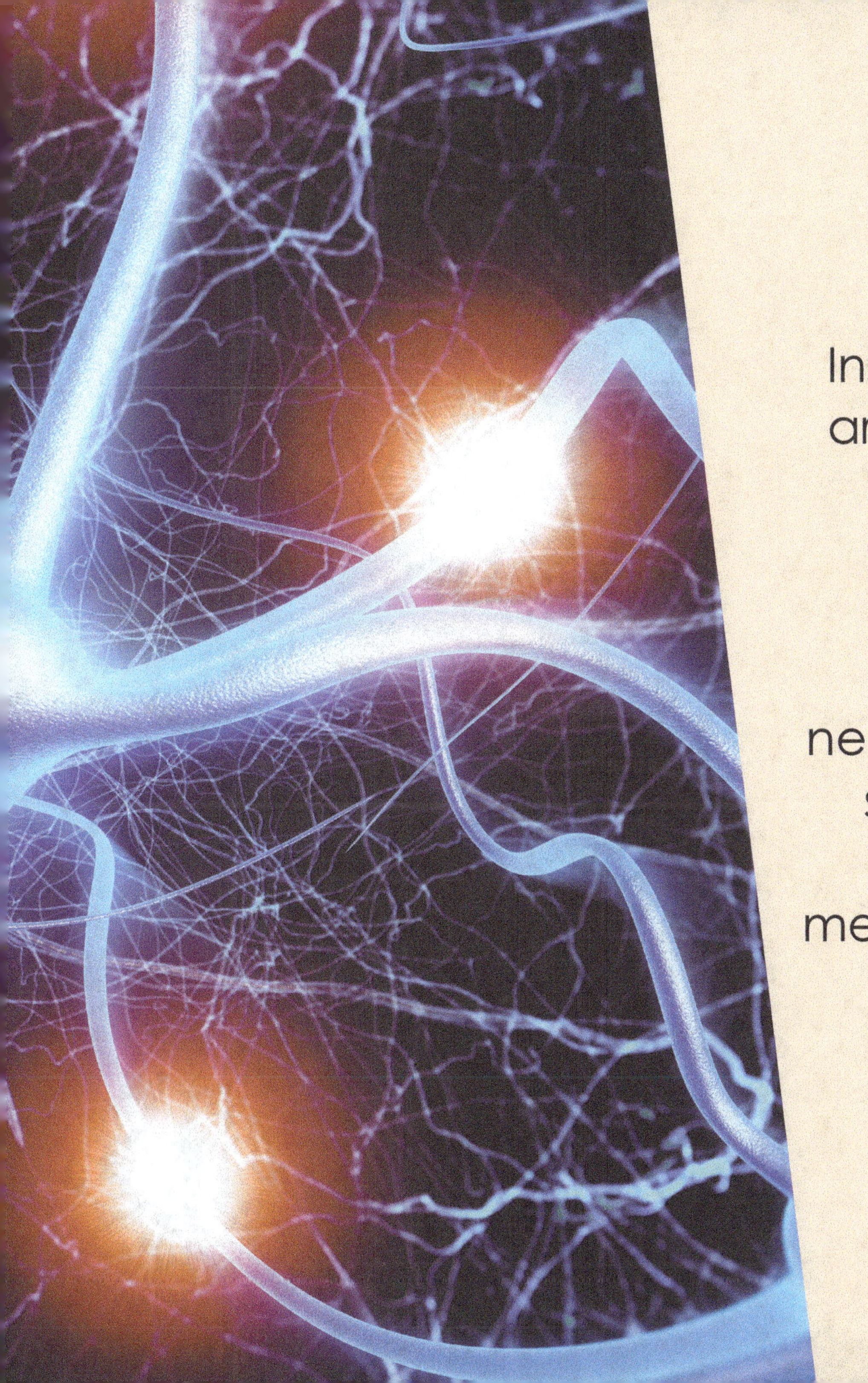

Inside your brain are microscopic cells called neurons. There are about 100 billion tiny, tiny neurons. Neurons send electrical and chemical messages to your body.

Neurons in your brain tell everything what to do. The neurons in one brain send more messages than all the phones in the entire world. They send information to your brain and carry messages from your brain to your body. Your brain never stops working.

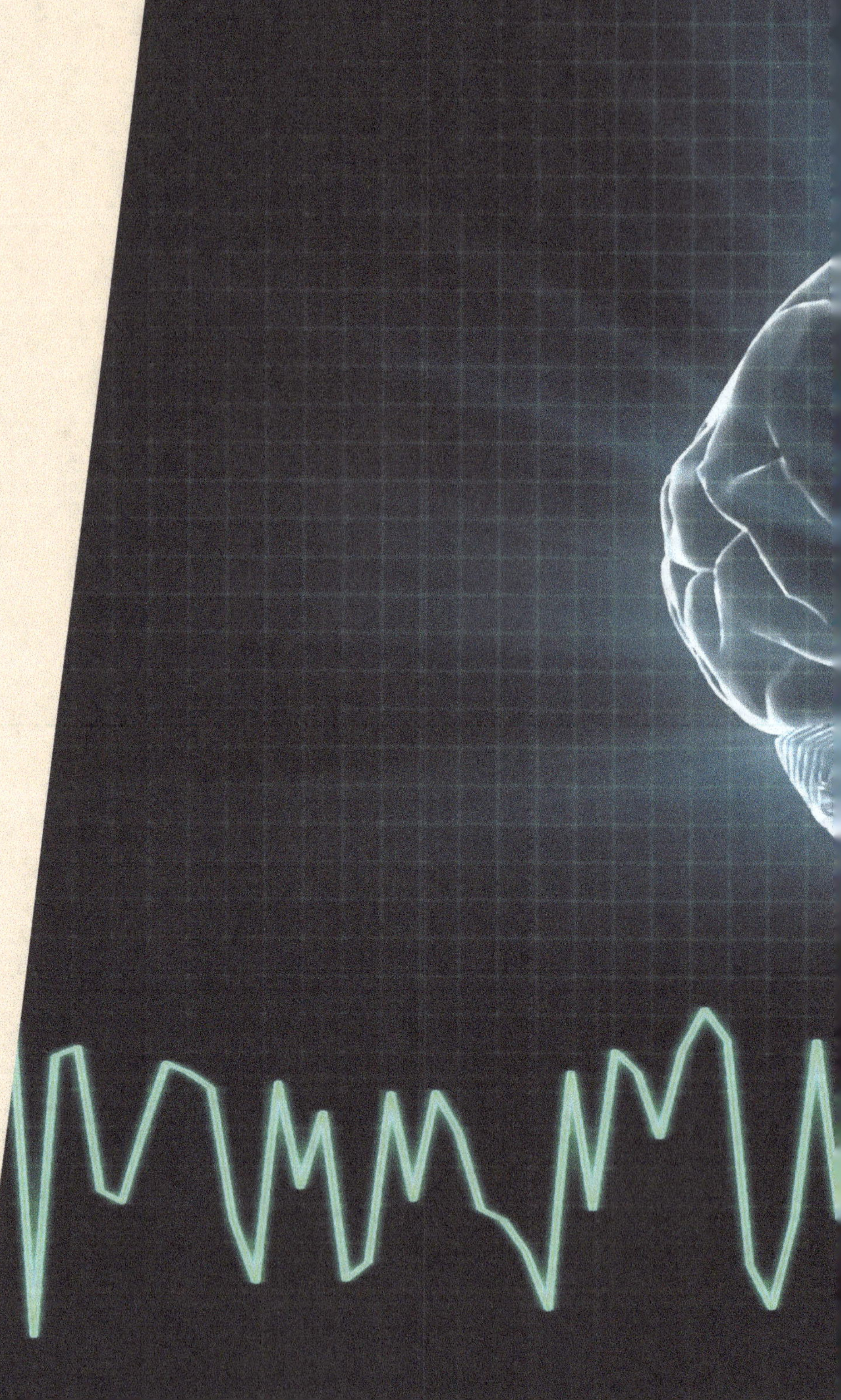

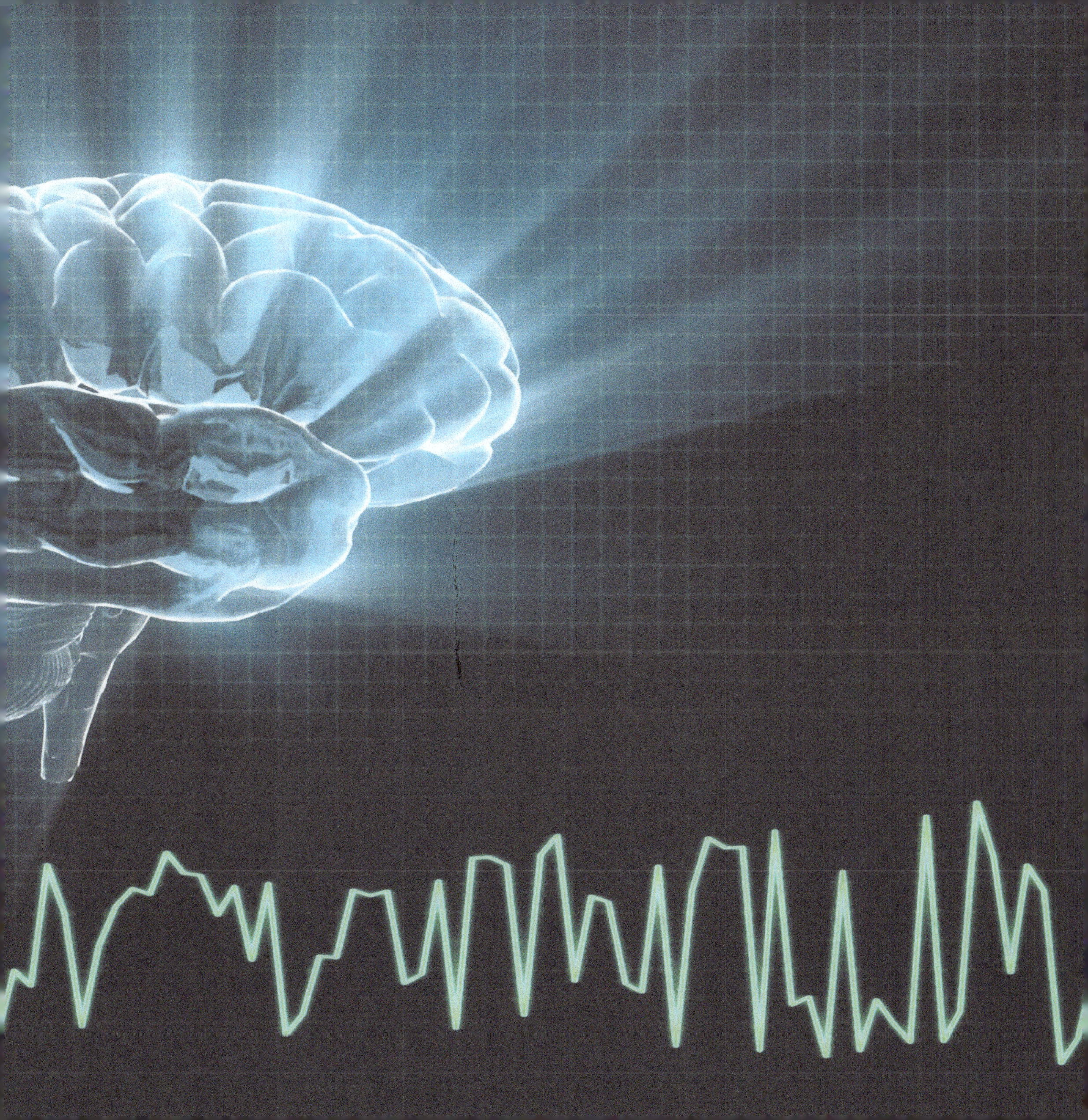

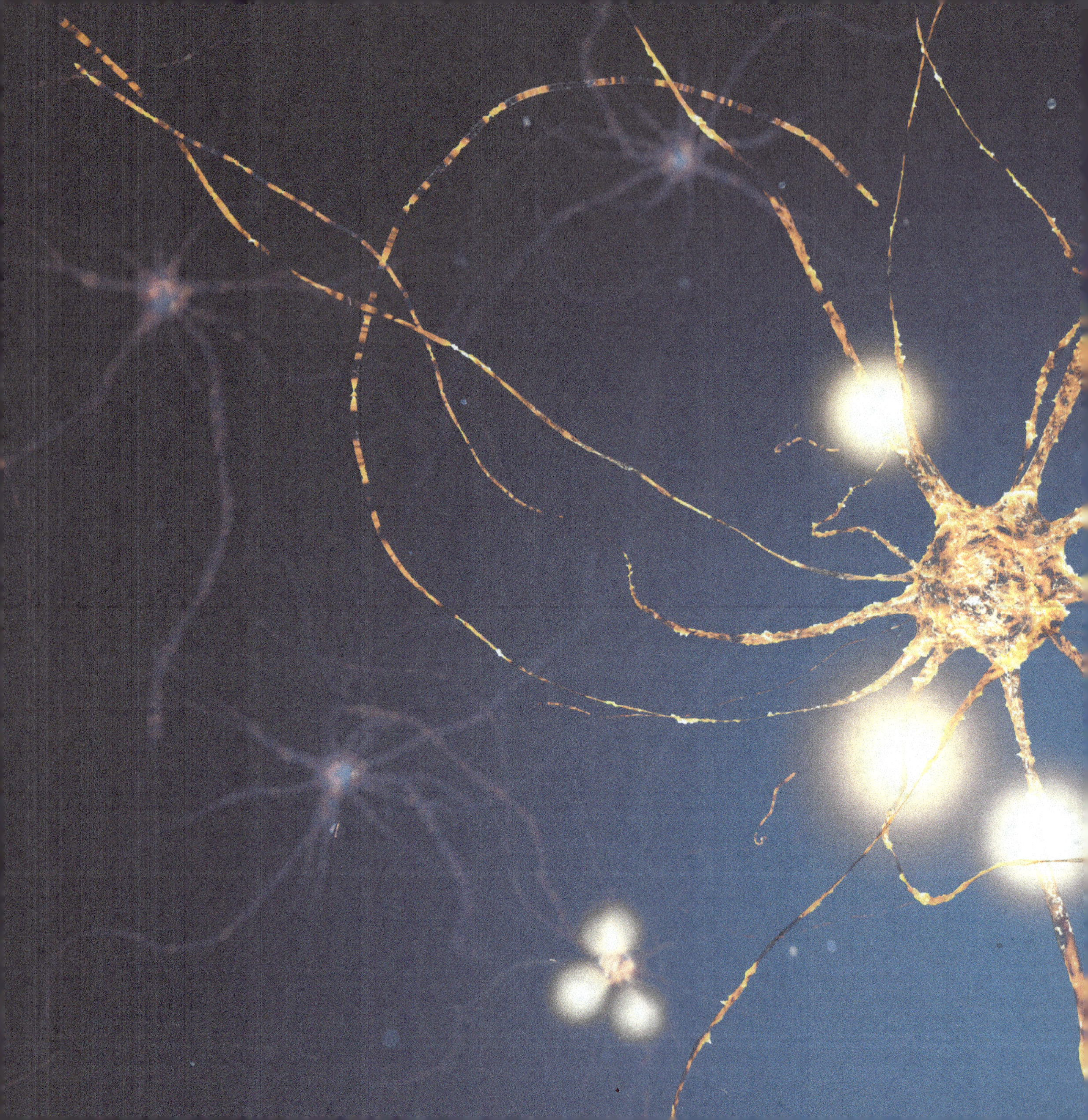

The neurons
in your brain
create
enough
electricity to
provide power
for a low-watt
light bulb. Your
neurons are
connected by
tiny pathways.
Exercise
can make
you smarter
because it
increases the
blood flow in
the brain.

Your brain has three main parts. The three parts work together. They are the cerebellum, cerebrum, and brain stem.

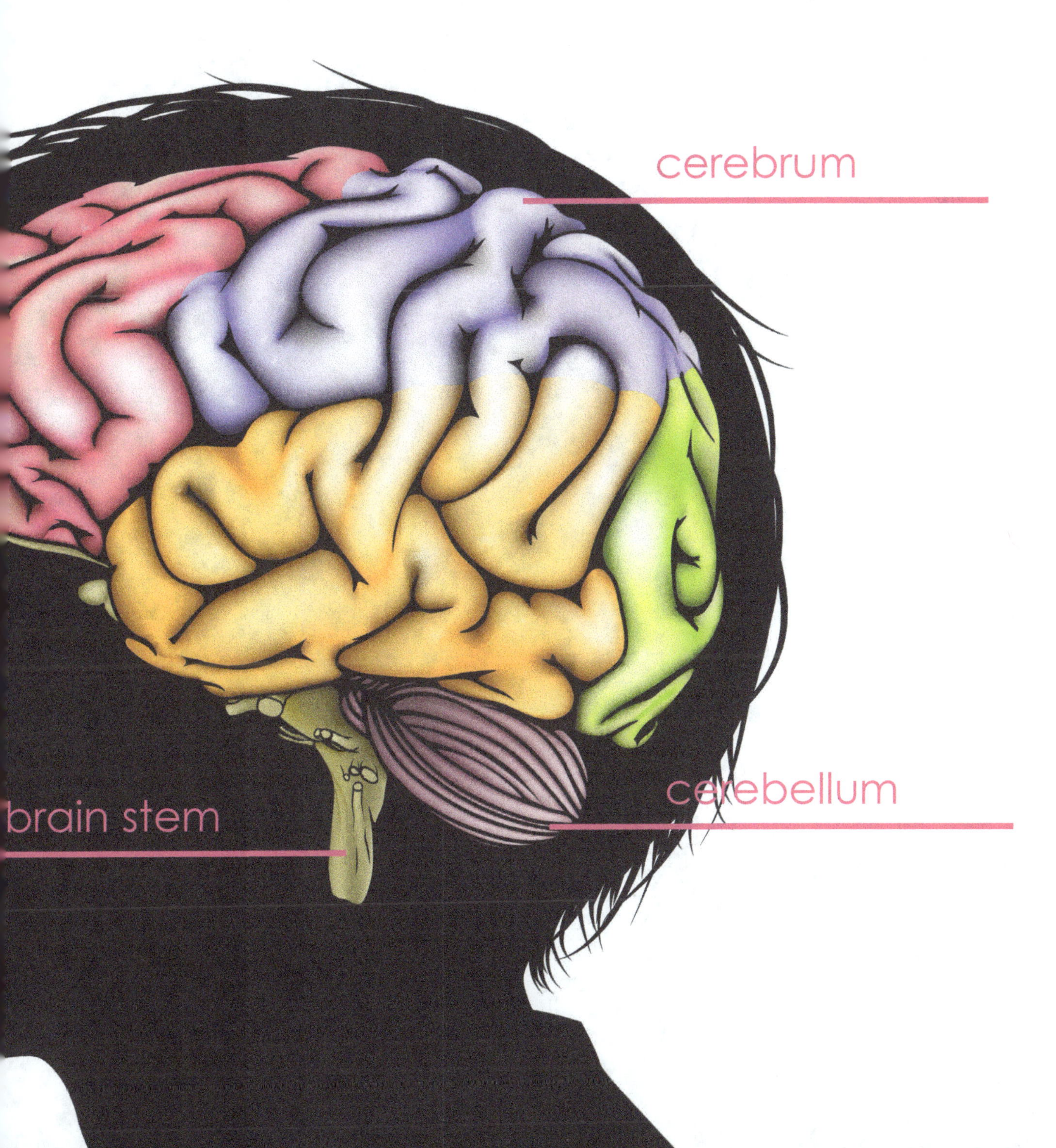

cerebrum
cerebellum
brain stem

The biggest part of the brain is the cerebrum (se-re-brum). The cerebrum makes up 85% of the brain's weight. It is the thinking part of the brain and it controls your voluntary muscles.

The cerebrum is divided into two halves. The right half helps you think like music, colors, and shapes. The left half tends to be more analytical, helping you with math, logic, and speech. The right side of the cerebrum controls the left side of your body, and the left side controls the right.

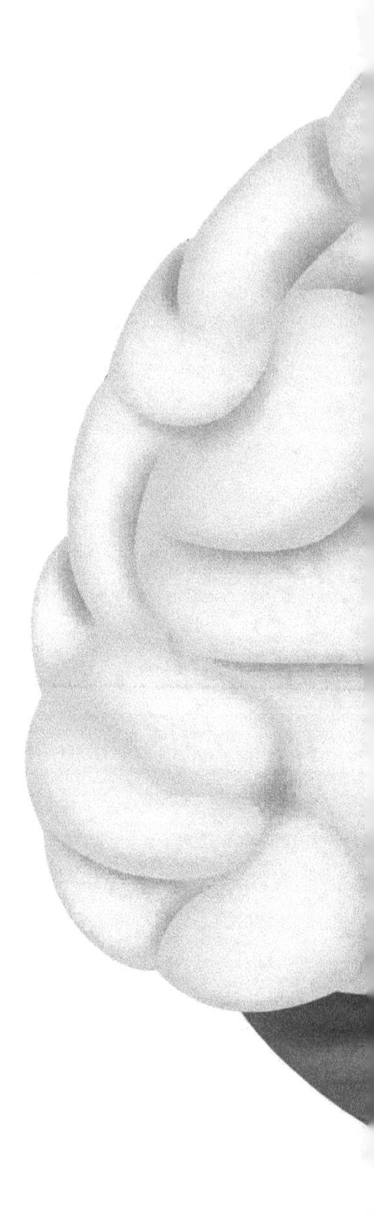

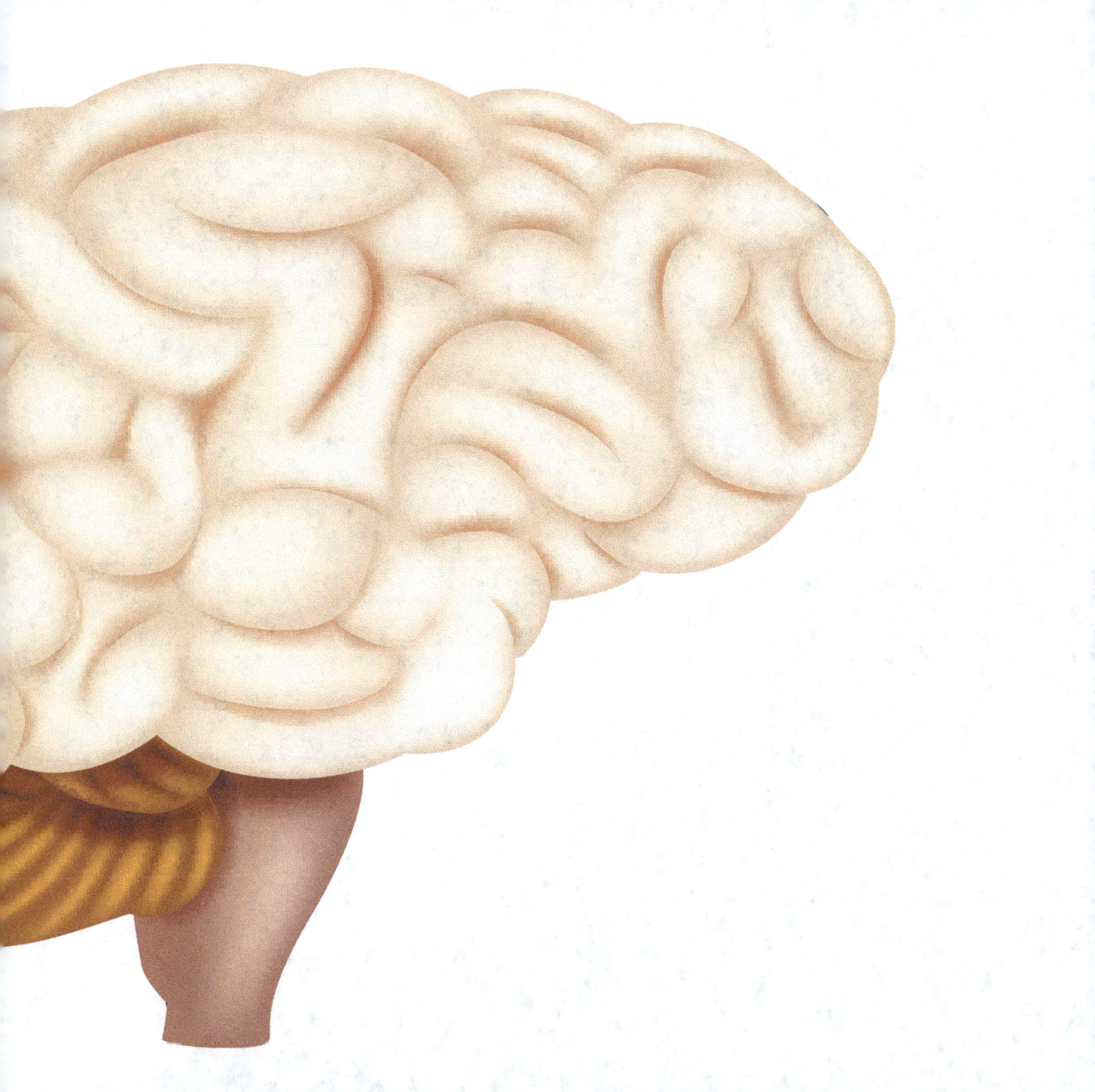

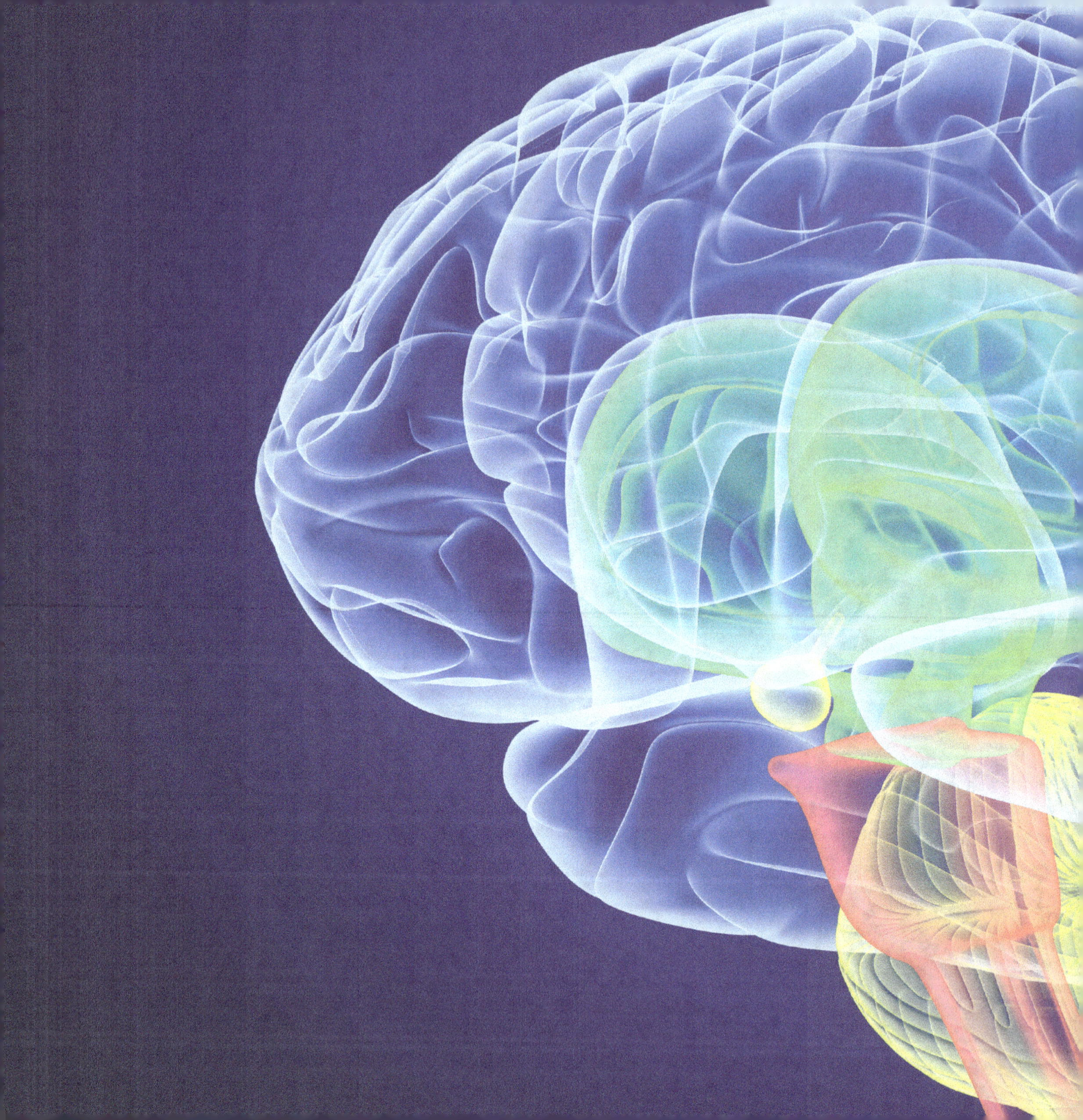

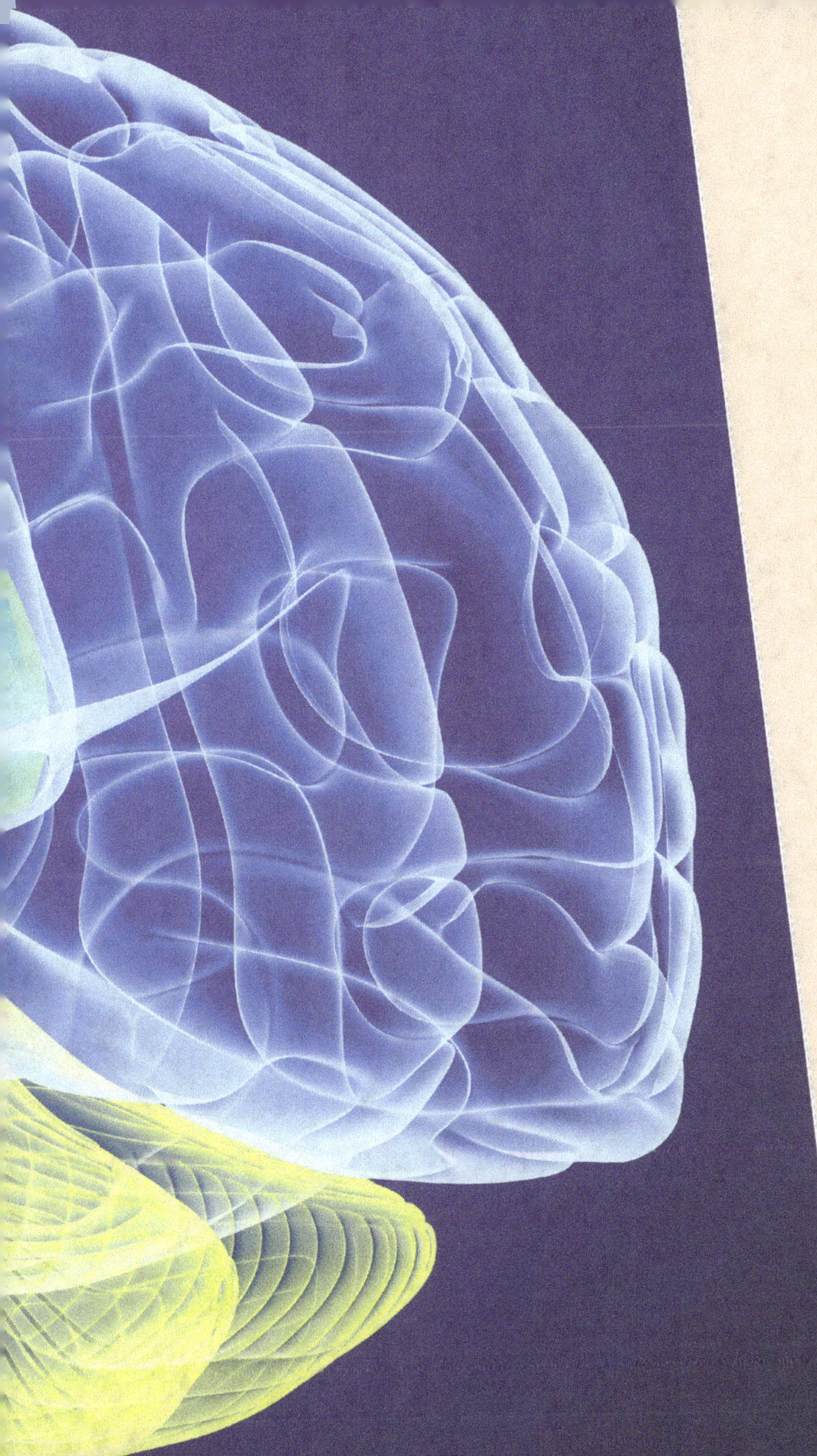

The cerebellum
(se-re-bell-um)
is located at
the back of
the brain. The
cerebellum
controls
balance,
movement, and
coordination.
It gives you the
ability to stand
upright, ride
on your bike or
cruise on your
skateboard.

The brain stem is a small part of the brain, but it is mighty. It connects your brain to your spinal cord and controls many automatic processes in your body. It is in charge of all the functions your body performs to stay alive, like breathing air, digesting food, and circulating blood.

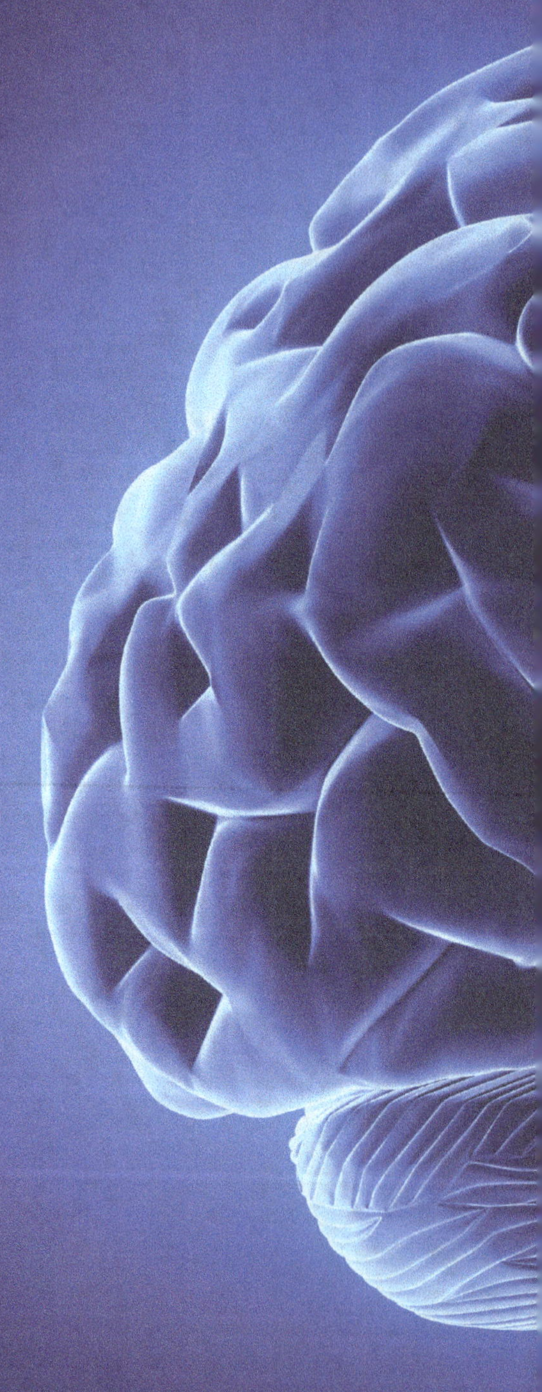

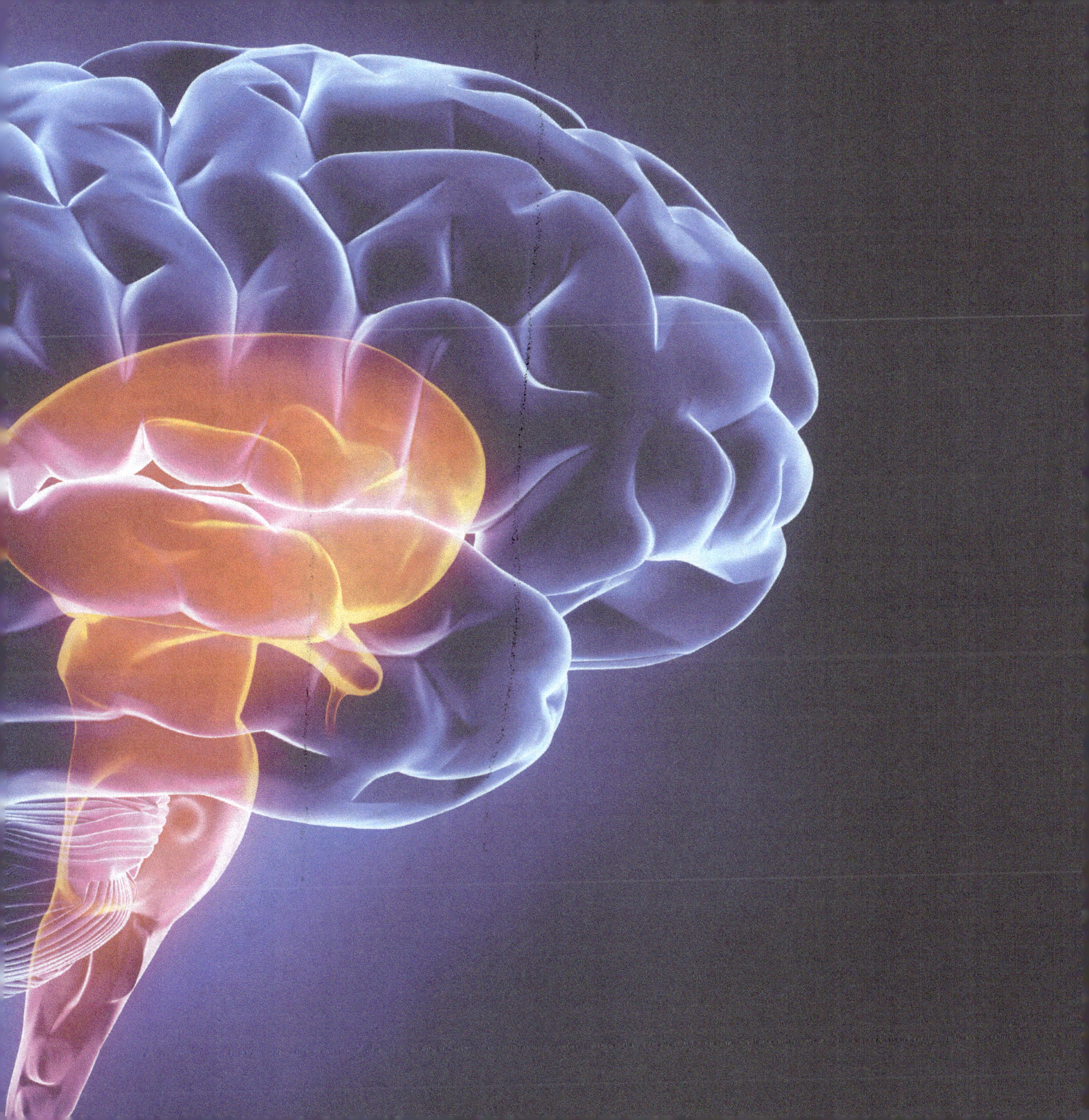

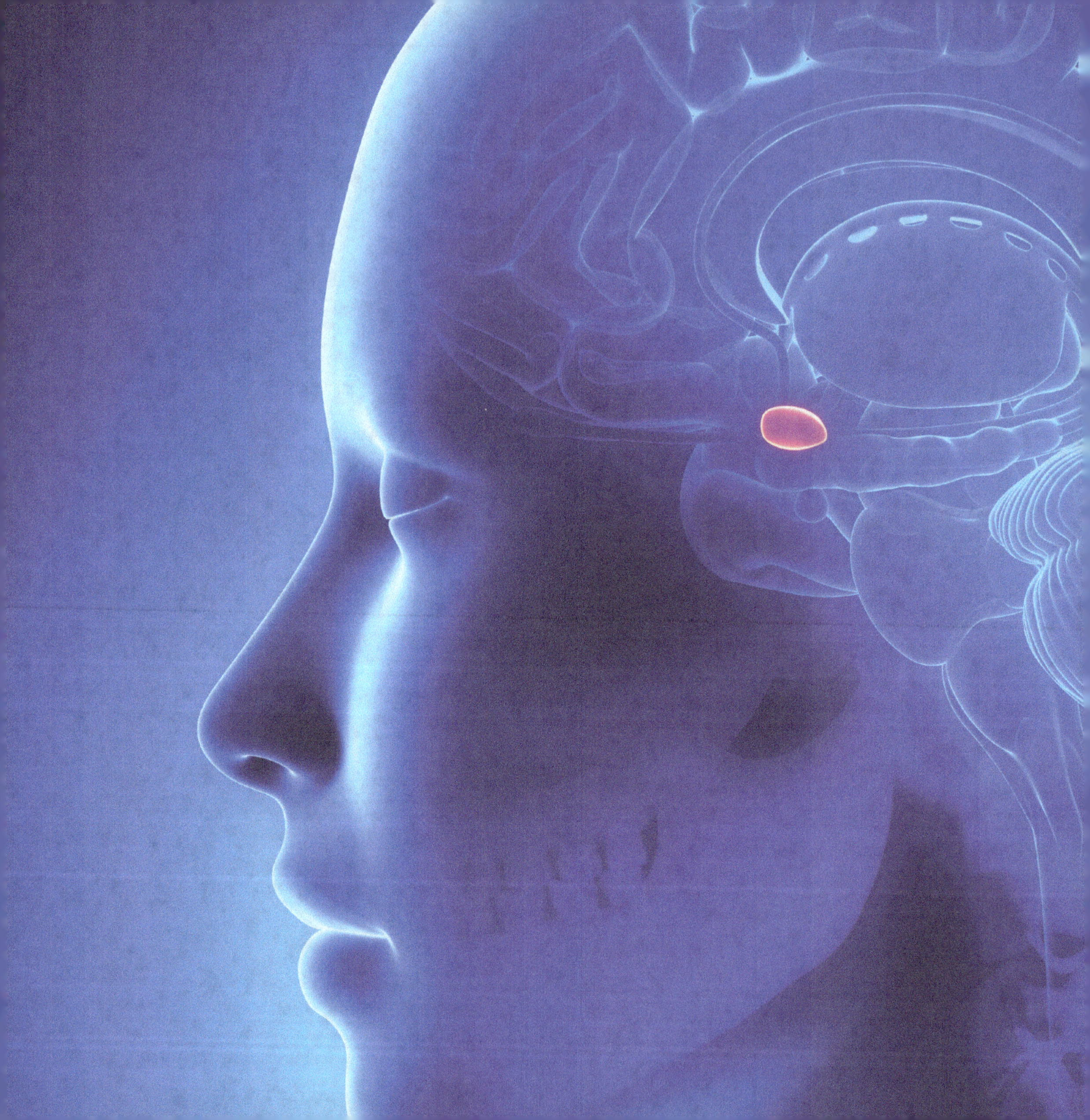

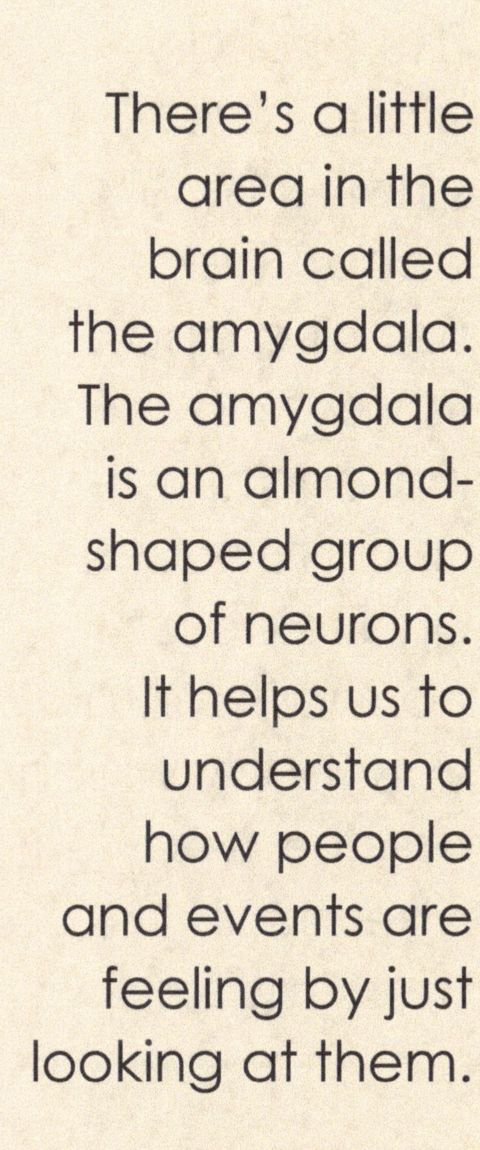

There's a little area in the brain called the amygdala. The amygdala is an almond-shaped group of neurons. It helps us to understand how people and events are feeling by just looking at them.

The pituitary
gland is very
small; it is only
about the
size of a pea.
It plays an
important role,
as it produces
and releases
hormones into
your body which
are the body's
chemical
messengers.

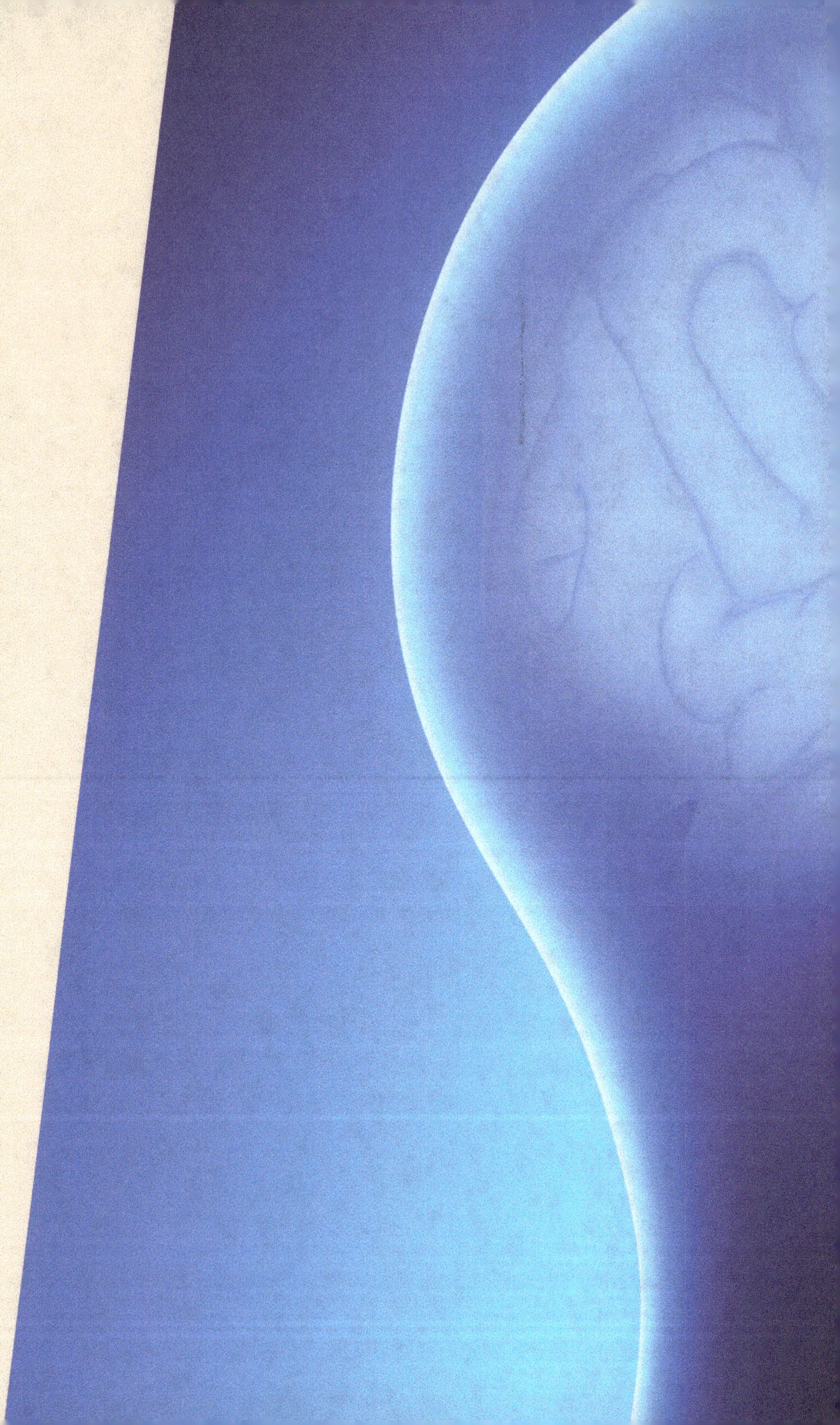

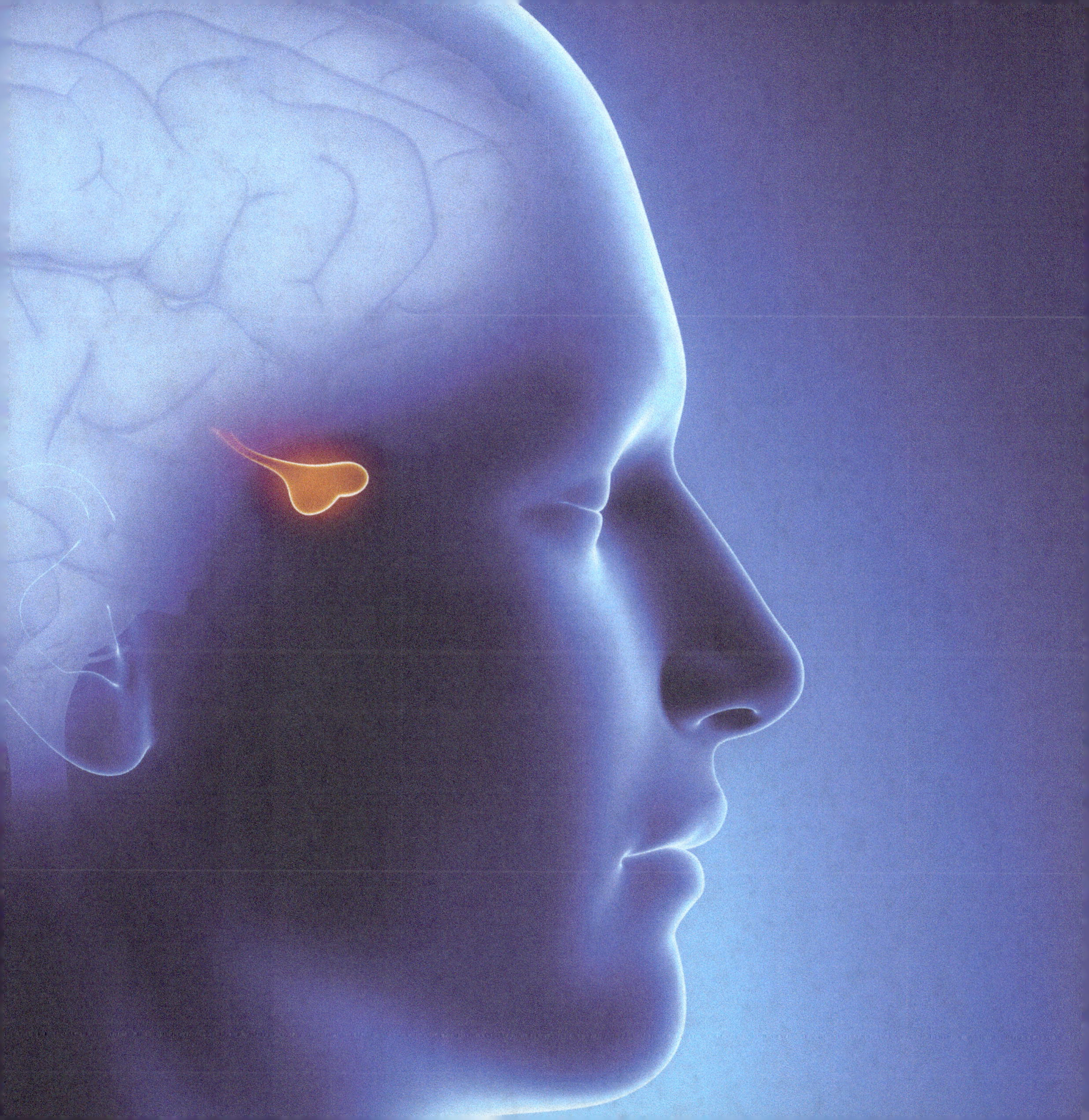

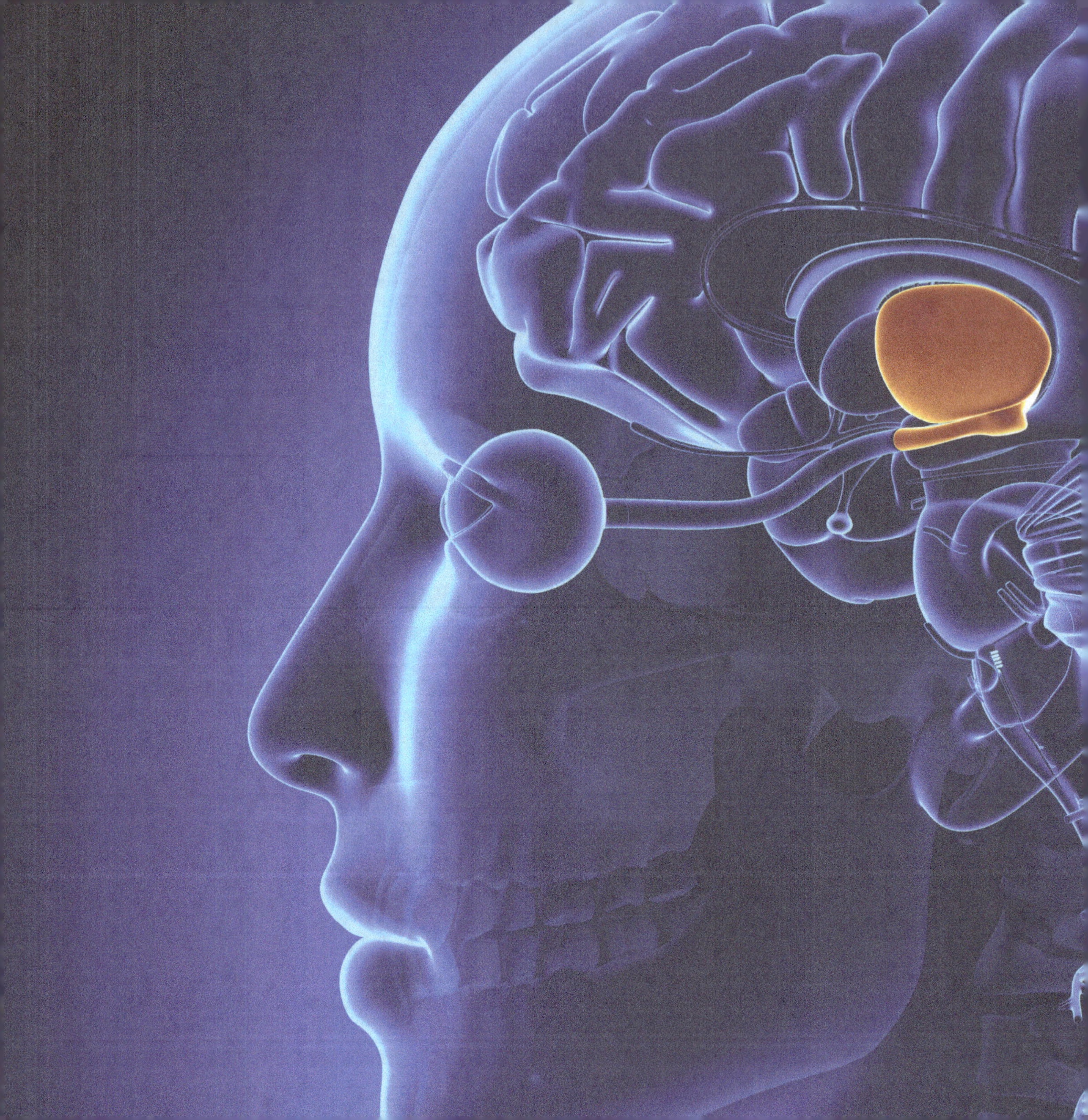

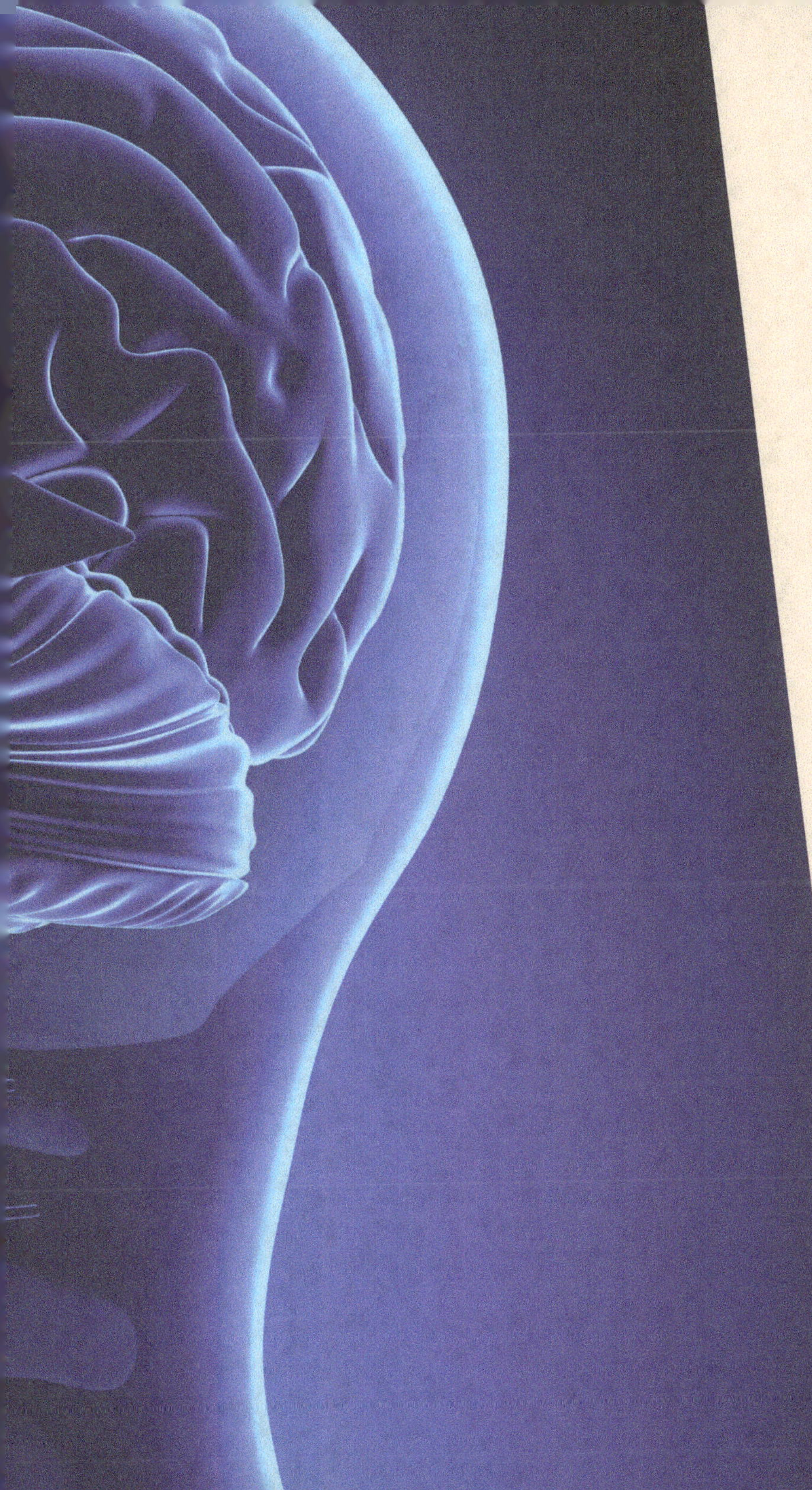

The
hypothalamus
is like your
brain's inner
thermostat. Your
hypothalamus
knows what
temperature
your body
should be. If
your body is
too hot, the
hypothalamus
tells it to sweat
and when
you're too cold
it tells your body
to shiver.

The corpus callosum is the band of white fibers that connects the cerebral hemispheres of your brain. It is right in the middle of your brain. It is also responsible for transmitting messages between the right and left sides of the brain.

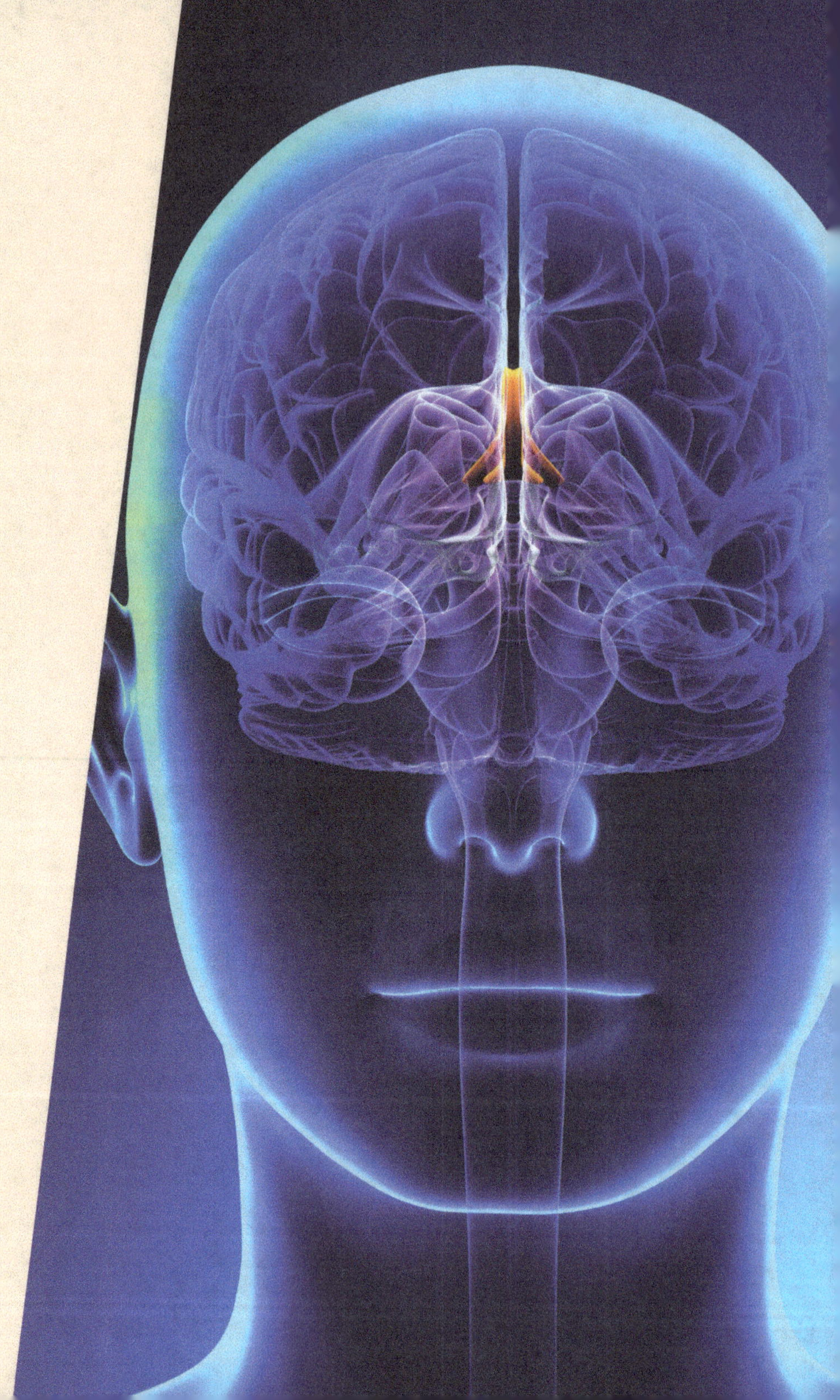

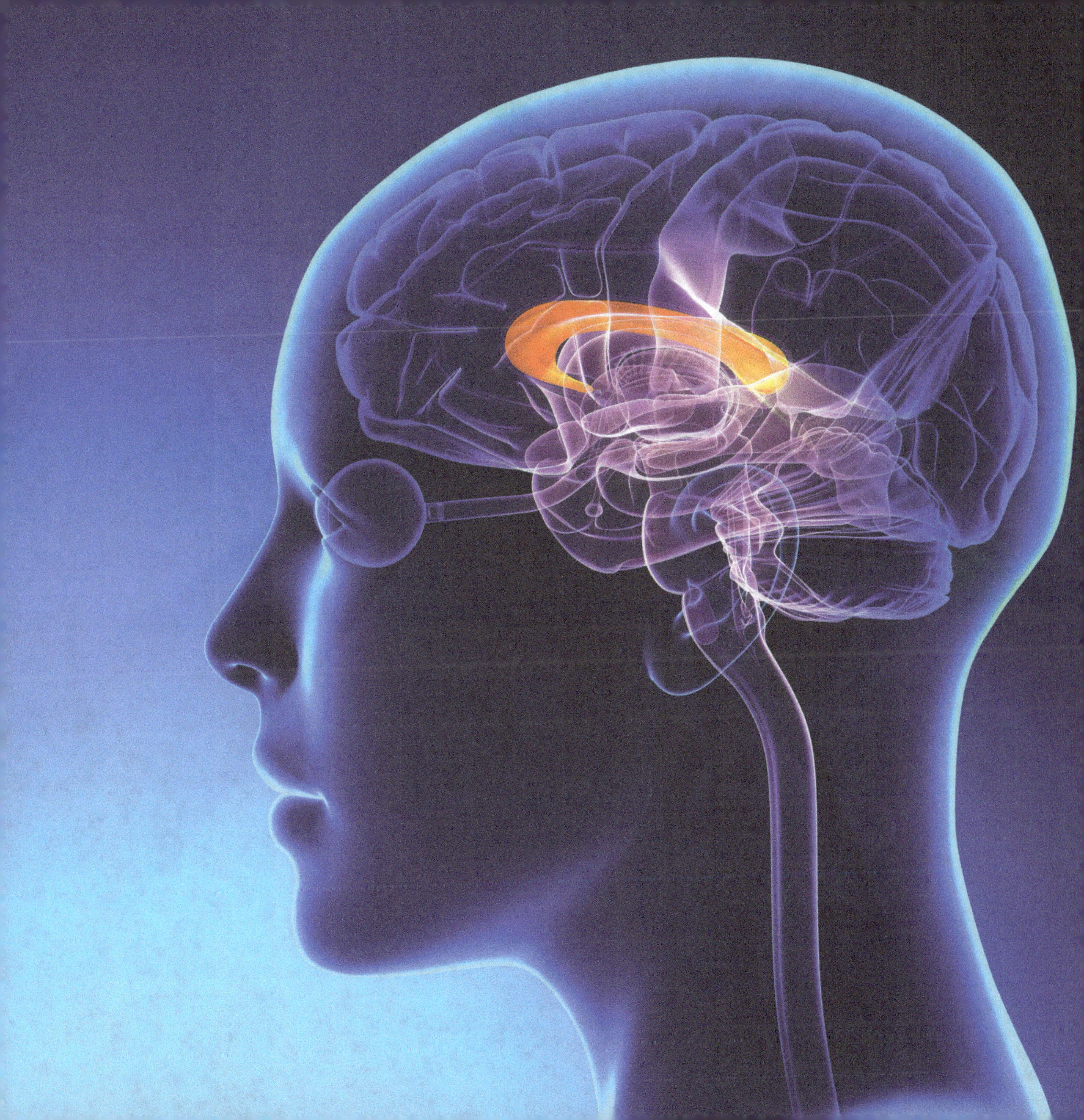

The brain is
about 60% fat.
It's a chubby
little organ.
The brain is
protected by
the skull, which
is made up of
22 bones that
are all joined
together.

Cranial nerves carry messages to and from the ears, eyes, nose, throat, tongue and skin on your face and scalp. There are 12 pairs of cranial nerves.

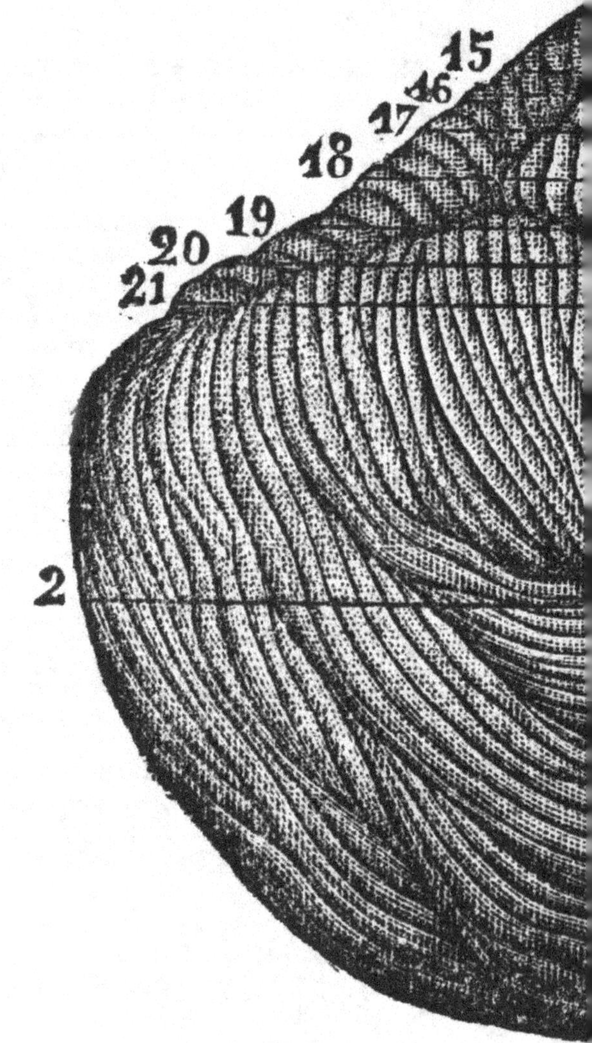

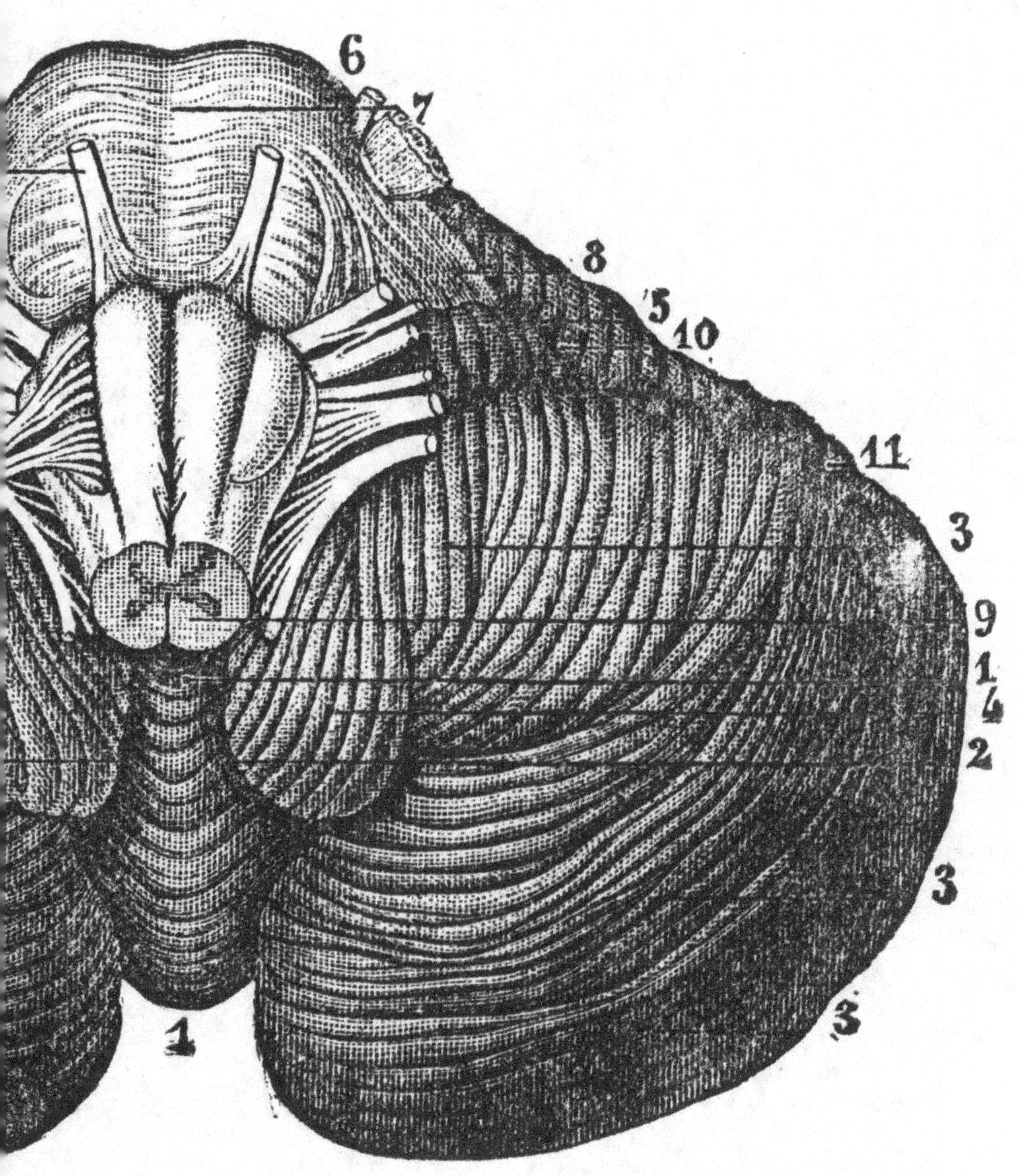

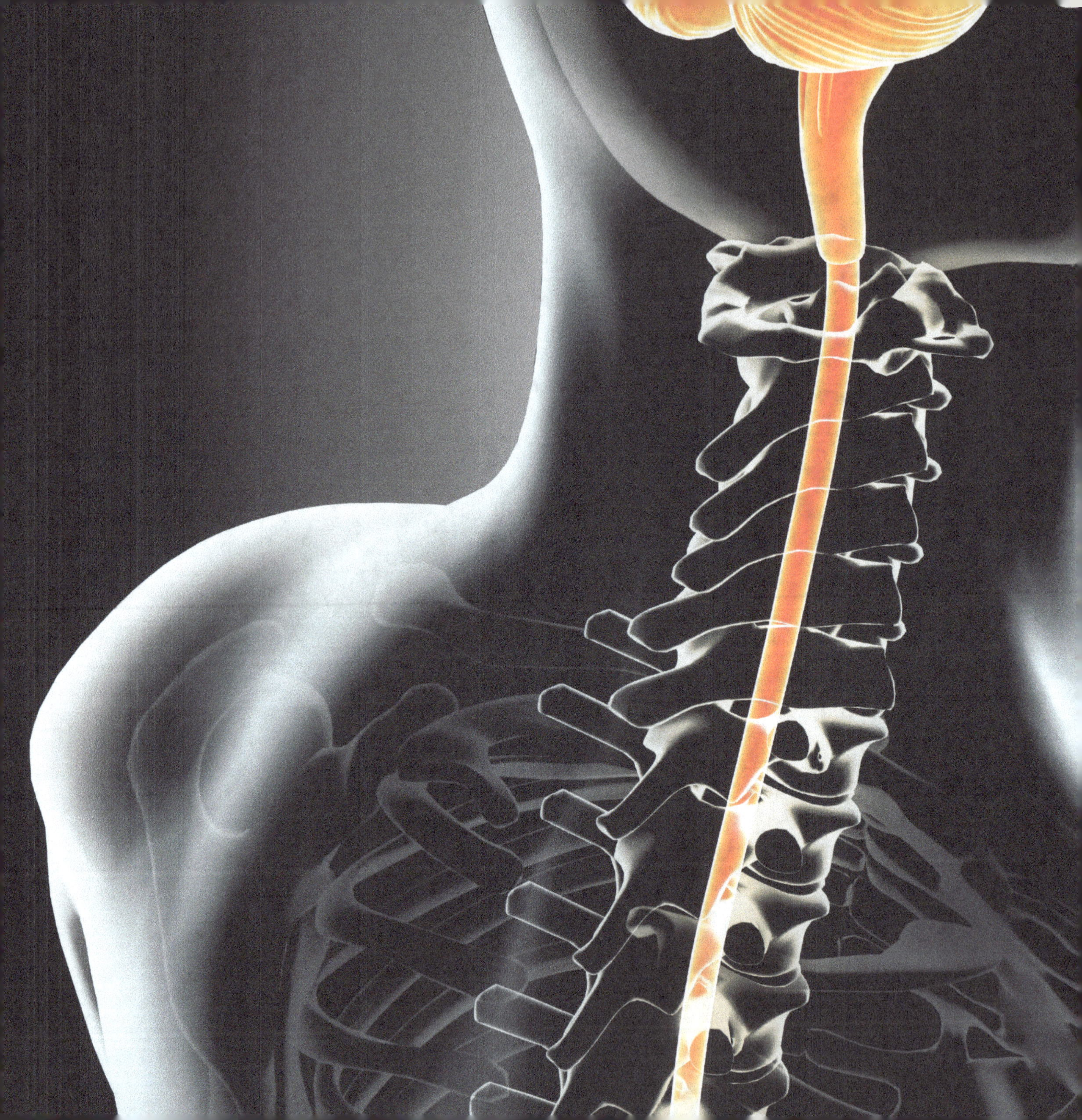

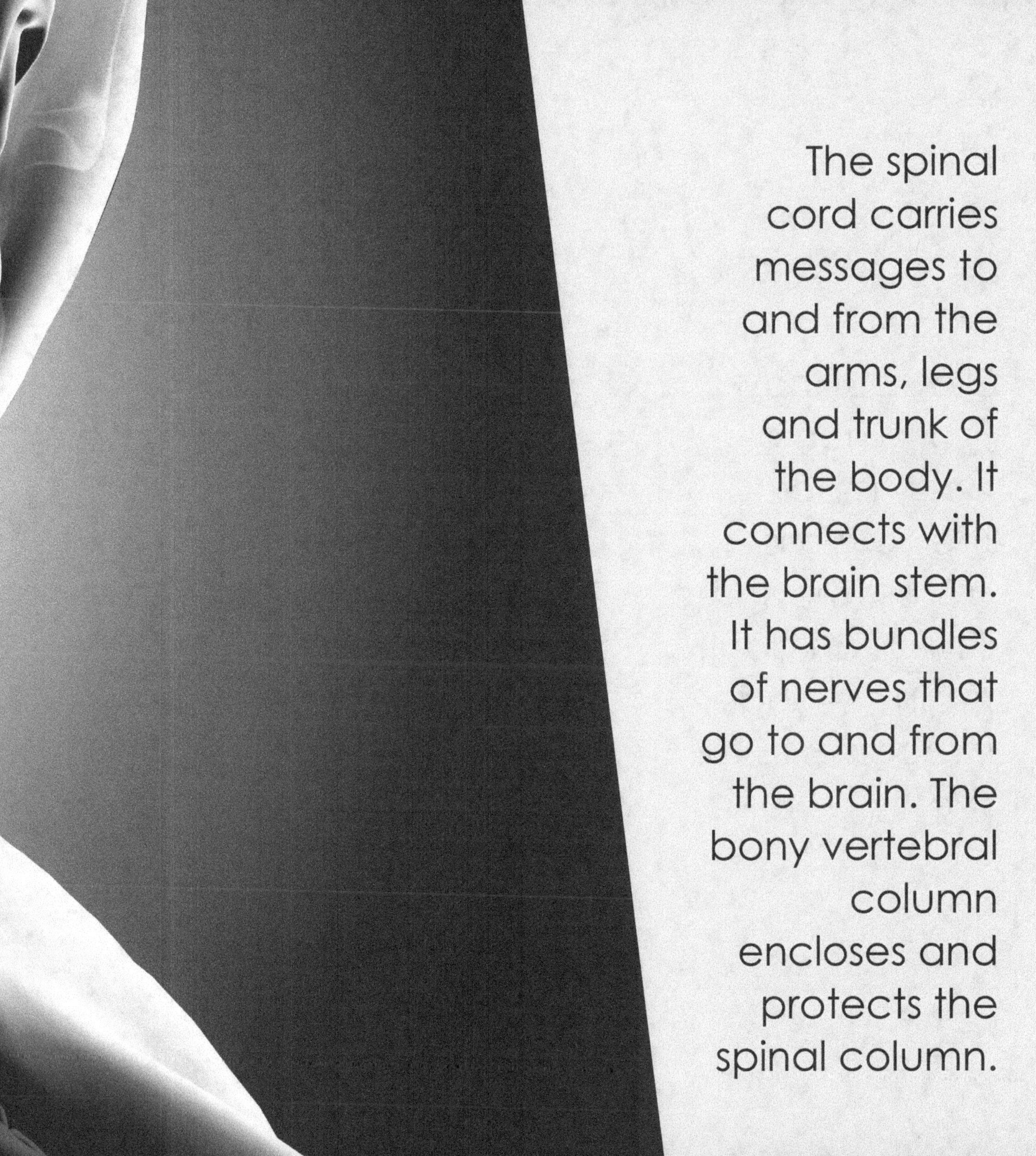
The spinal
cord carries
messages to
and from the
arms, legs
and trunk of
the body. It
connects with
the brain stem.
It has bundles
of nerves that
go to and from
the brain. The
bony vertebral
column
encloses and
protects the
spinal column.

Did you know
that when a
baby is born,
their brain is
almost the same
size as an adult
brain? At age 6
it reaches its full
size.

Potassium and calcium are the two minerals important for the nervous system. You must eat plenty of healthy foods to keep your brain healthy.

Do challenging
activities, such
as puzzles,
reading, playing
music, making
art, or anything
else that gives
your brain a
workout. This
way you can
use your brain
and keeps it
working well.

Make sure you get enough sleep. Sleep helps your brain to remember all your memories. When you're dreaming your brainwaves are more active than when you're awake.

Visit
BABY PROFESSOR
EDUCATION KIDS
www.BabyProfessorBooks.com
to download Free Baby Professor eBooks
and view our catalog of new and exciting
Children's Books

www.ingramcontent.com/pod-product-compliance
Lightning Source LLC
Chambersburg PA
CBHW081355150726
48196CB00005BA/504